ONE SHOW INTERACTIVE

VOLUME VIII . Advertising's Best Interactive and New Media

President

David Baldwin

Executive Director

Mary Warlick

Marketing Director/Editor

Kevin Swanepoel

Editor

Maiko Shiratori

Contributing Editor

Matt Helland

Steve Marchese

Yash Egami

Designer

Jennah Synnestvedt

**Cover and Divider Page Design/
DVD Production**

Joshua Davis

Joshua Davis Studios/Mineola

Published by

One Club Publishing LLC

21 E. 26th Street, 5th Floor

New York, NY 10010

Tel: +1 (212) 979 1900

Fax: +1 (212) 979 50.06

Email: publishing@oneclub.org

Web: www.oneclub.org

In Association with The One Club

First Printing

ISBN: 0-929837-28-2

Production and Separation

AVA Book Production Pte. Ltd.

E-mail: production@avabooks.com.sg

Distribution (USA and International)

Rockport Publishers

3 Commercial Street

Gloucester, MA 01930, USA

Web: www.rockpub.com

Sponsors

Media Temple

Yahoo!

INTRODUCTION

PENCIL WINNERS

MERIT WINNERS

INDEX

THE ONE CLUB

THE ONE CLUB

Based in New York City, The One Club was founded in 1975 and is a non-profit organization dedicated to maintaining the highest standards of creativity in advertising. Its 1,000 members include many of advertising's most respected art directors and copywriters, as well as students of advertising.

MISSION

As part of its mission to promote high standards of creative excellence, The One Club produces the advertising industry's most prestigious awards program, The One Show. Judged by a panel of the advertising industry's elite creative directors, this annual event acknowledges excellence in art direction, design, and copywriting in a variety of categories, including television, radio, newspapers, magazines, billboards and public service. The coveted One Show "Gold Pencils" are regarded as the zenith of achievement in the advertising world.

In 1998, The One Club launched One Show Interactive, the first awards show dedicated exclusively to advertising in new media. With the One Show Interactive awards, The One Club extended its mission of recognizing creative excellence to the new media field.

PROGRAMS

The One Club regularly produces a variety of events and programs that encourage aspiring advertising professionals to hone their craft. These programs include:

- "Gold on Gold" Lectures (award-winning industry professionals discussing the creative process)

- Portfolio Reviews

- One Show College Competition

- Creative Workshops

- one.a magazine—a quarterly publication by and for advertising creatives

- One Club Gallery Exhibitions

- Traveling One Show Exhibitions

- The One Show Annual, the indispensable hard cover reference showcasing the best advertising worldwide

- One Show Interactive Annual, the first book of its kind, highlighting the best new media advertising

EDUCATION

In 1995, The One Club established an educational department, dedicated to fostering the creative talents of advertising students nationwide. The department sponsors educational programs and events, and administers scholarships to outstanding students in advertising programs at a select number of colleges and advertising schools throughout the country.

DAVID BALDWIN
President // The One Club

Welcome to the 2005 One Show Interactive.

It has been a great year for interactive work. Which is to say it has been a great year for great ideas. After all, we don't work in an industry of mediums, we work in a business of problem solving with ideas that make people think, act, engage and maybe even see things differently.

I guess more to the point, as you look at this year's winners you'll see ideas that are sometimes hard to pin down as merely interactive. Often they are the interactive component of a much bigger idea. Or they're the pointy end of something bigger.

In fact, from a judging perspective, we saw a lot of the same work entered and represented in both the One Show and the One Show Interactive. You just can't draw a clean line between where an idea stops in one medium and begins in another.

We live in an age when designers do interactive, interactive people do advertising and advertising people do interactive.

Just look at Burger King's Chicken Fight campaign. Was it a TV idea? An online idea? An online game? An in-store idea? A TV show? The answer of course is yes to all of these.

Possibly more germane is that, like a lot of work today, this idea isn't whole except when expressed in all of the categories. The whole is much bigger than the parts, but the parts are still delightful unto themselves.

Or how about Converse Gallery? One of the more interesting ways to involve and create loyalists to a brand I've seen in a very long time. Not to mention an interesting way to use interactive to create great television, outdoor and other offline advertising. I was going to say "traditional" advertising but somehow that word doesn't feel right. Maybe we need to invent a new one.

Our Best of Show, Burger King's Subservient Chicken comes to mind as well. Again a groundbreaking piece on its own, but really part of a much bigger idea.

For those of you wondering, entries were up 25% over last year hailing from 34 countries.

All the usual places were represented, of course, but then so were countries like China, Sweden, Argentina, Denmark, Korea, the Netherlands, Malaysia, the Russian Federation, the Dominican Republic and the Czech Republic just to name more than a few.

So crack this book open and take a look. There's a whole world inside.

THE ONE CLUB

KEVIN SWANEPOEL

Marketing & Interactive Director // The One Club

"If you aren't doing interactive, you'd better get out of the ad business."

It's a strong statement, but it's one I hear often from leading creatives, and I believe it accurately reflects where our industry is headed as we celebrate nine years of One Show Interactive, advertising's premier interactive awards show.

Interactive advertising has reached a turning point. It began as an afterthought when Arnold Worldwide launched a Web site to support its multimillion-dollar print and television campaign for Volkswagen Beetle, and evolved years later into Fallon Worldwide's groundbreaking online work for BMW. This year, interactive has moved into the forefront, confirmed by Crispin Porter + Bogusky's ubiquitous "Subservient Chicken" viral promotion for Burger King.

Today, clients are demanding that the Web become the nucleus around which an entire campaign is built. The reasons are obvious. No other medium offers instant feedback, facts on sales and market share, and the ability to track ROI and adjust strategies to fit consumer preferences. It is dynamic, instantaneous, and—just as important—its reach is virtually unlimited.

This presents challenges to both traditional and interactive agencies. You can't just take a television commercial, throw it on the Web, and hope it will get e-mailed around. A successful interactive campaign demands smart, engaging content that will entice users to visit and pass it on. The interactive medium is driven by users seeking out content that is both relevant and interesting. Users "pull" content, and certainly shy away from bland, uninteresting content that is "pushed" at them.

This year, One Show Interactive received over 1,500 entries from 34 countries worldwide. In the approaching years, I expect The One Club will receive even more entries from more countries as interactive flourishes and is regarded as a mainstream medium rather than a fringe or supplemental tool to reach consumers.

DOUG JAEGER
One Show Interactive Jury Chairman
President, Creative Director
thehappycorp.com, New York

Every year computers get faster, screens get bigger, more people get broadband connections. And every year this book becomes more important. There are a lot of people to thank for that and there are a lot of those people's mothers and fathers to thank as well. This is just one more stop on our way to the future. We can count the number of years on our own hands when the first sentence of this paragraph will be as outdated as the idea of printing this book.

We are in a year when blogs give major media companies a case of identity crisis, putting the word IP before telephony begins to scare even the largest telephone companies, and SPAM is still something that people are trying to avoid on the computer and at the dinner table. Today, brands start to look at their feathered friends on the Internet to provide answers to their marketing problems. We are at the beginning again.

Let's take you back to earth. You are looking at a book where there is a picture of me above these feeble letters. I am asked here to write a letter from the interactive chair. I am meant to give perspective on this great book you are about to explore. It's a rare glimpse at the still frames of the animated and interactive works only to be brought to life on millions of computers worldwide.

In this book you will find a collection of work judged by an elite panel of the world's highest paid, most talented and experienced members of the creative digital advertising community. I give you this opportunity to peruse a time capsule, as it features this year's finest pieces of interactive marketing and communication.

JUDGES' CHOICE

INTERACTIVE JUDGES

DOUG JAEGER (Chair)
thehappycorp.com/New York

KEITH ANDERSON
Goodby, Silverstein & Partners/
San Francisco

LARS BASTHOLM
AKQA/New York

ANNA COLL
DoubleYou/Barcelona

FABIO COSTA
BlastRadius/Toronto

JOSHUA DAVIS
Joshua Davis Studios/Mineola

RICARDO FIGUEIRA
AgenciaClick/São Paulo

CHRIS FRANZESE
hanft raboy and partners/New York

SEAN PATRICK GANANN
NetX/Balmain, Australia

FOLKERT GORTER
Newstoday/Amsterdam

CHRISTIAN HAAS
Organic/San Francisco

NATHAN HACKSTOCK
TEQUILA\Los Angeles

ROB HUDAK
Freelance/New York

MAYA KOPYTMAN
IconNicholson/New York

KEN-ICHI KUBO
NEC Media Products/Tokyo

SASHA KURTZ
Dotglu/New York

MICHAEL KUTSCHINSKI
OgilvyInteractive/Frankfurt

EARNEST LUPINACCI
Anomaly/New York

SIMON MILLISHIP
Wunderman Interactive/London

TOKE NYGAARD
Cuban Council/New York

NAOTO OIWA
Dentsu/Tokyo

MATIAS PALM-JENSEN
Farfar/Stockholm

ROBERT RASMUSSEN
Wieden + Kennedy/Portland

ED ROBINSON
Viral Factory/London

FERNANDA ROMANO
DM9DDB/São Paulo

NIK ROOPE
Poke/London

TOM ROOPE
tomato/London

PAULO SANNA
OgilvyInteractive/New York

MICHAEL VOLKMER
Scholz & Volkmer/Wiesbaden

BRIGITTE VON PUTTKAMER
Framfab/Munich

STEVE VRANAKIS
VCCP/London

佐々木康晴 Sasaki,Yasuharu   Interactive Director
勉強と釣りと動物とPCと徹夜が趣味。転覆隊隊員。
Being a student of life, Fishing, loving animals,
and pulling "all-nighters"are his passion. | Back |

JUDGES' CHOICE

Interactive Salaryman . CLIENT // Dentsu (Interactive Salaryman)
ANNUAL ID // 05047N

KEITH ANDERSON
Goodby, Silverstein & Partners/San Francisco

"As you know, 'salaryman' is a certain Japanese businessman who works hard, always quiet, serious, and looks a little bit odd. Their work is also odd, but sometimes sparkling."

Maybe it was the site description above, or maybe it was my long buried attraction to pop guns, or maybe it was really just the innate fashion sense displayed on the site. Whatever it was, interactivesalaryman.com was one of the few sites that really stood out for me this year. It captured a personality completely and effortlessly. It was easy to digest and well produced. It stayed true to its intent, and its design vision.

The design was arresting and unexpected. The execution was flawless. And for a portfolio site it was entertaining and informative. It had a level of interaction that was engaging but did not become overly complex.

And perhaps most importantly, it didn't take itself too seriously.

Feature Technology

ロケットの速さに匹敵する

is to a space shuttle

it

Making of 'it'

PAUSE

BGM : A Whole New World ○ #1 ● #2

RESET

BACK

it

JUDGES' CHOICE

It . CLIENT // NEC Corporation + ANNUAL ID // 05168N

LARS BASTHOLM
AKQA/New York

My favorite piece of work this year never made it past the Merit stage. The great Japanese
agency Dentsu's project for NEC called "It" manages to combine technology, storytelling
and interactivity in a novel and engaging way. It's a 45-minute sci-fi movie that incorporates
many of NEC's cutting-edge technologies to drive the plot forward. But it's also a fascinating
approach to product presentations and corporate image building. I think we're all looking
for the optimal way of integrating video and interactivity, and while the "It" site does not solve
that particular challenge, it is an interesting attempt at something new.

JUDGES' CHOICE

Toshiba Presents FM Festival 2004
CLIENT // Toshiba Corporation, Tokyo FM Broadcasting
ANNUAL ID // 05025N

ANNA COLL
DoubleYou/Barcelona

How many music portals have you visited and how many were like this one? The Toshiba Presents FM Festival 2004 Web site shows a great deal of content and information in a really elegant, smart and intuitive way. At the same time, the tone is both emotional and dynamic, making it a very funky site perfectly suited to the young audience it addresses. Awesome.

FOLKERT GORTER
Newstoday/Amsterdam

It's obvious that Yugo Nakamura had a big hand in the conception, design and development of FM Festival '04, a "visible radio station" that broadcasted independent music by artists throughout Japan. I particularly like this project because of its innovative approach to the medium: the seamless usage of multimedia like audio, video, animation and interface behaviors, which were combined effortlessly into an immersive experience that not only functions the way you expect, but surprises you with each visit. It doesn't happen often that an ambitious concept like this is actually developed and published. I believe this project is particularly successful for its uncompromising quality: It was executed with a great eye and feel for detail and was obviously created out of love for the medium more than for the actual brief, client or money. A great example—I'd even called it a definition—of "Web-based design" by people who love what they do and do what they love.

JUDGES' CHOICE

Kick Your Mouse . CLIENT // PUMA + ANNUAL ID // 05092N

FABIO COSTA
BlastRadius/Toronto

You mean aside from Burger King's Subservient Chicken? The most memorable work for me is without a doubt the PUMA Ultimate Football Simulator in the Beyond-the-Banner category. The idea to literally kick your mouse to play this game is so absurd that it makes it odd, funny and challenging.

Maybe the execution could have been art directed a little bit better, but this idea really resonates for me.

KEN-ICHI KUBO
NEC Media Products/Tokyo

The most important thing in interactive advertising is how to exceed the limitation of browser size. This work proposes the answer with a unique sense of humor and lovable trick.

Fortunately, my mouse did not blow out.

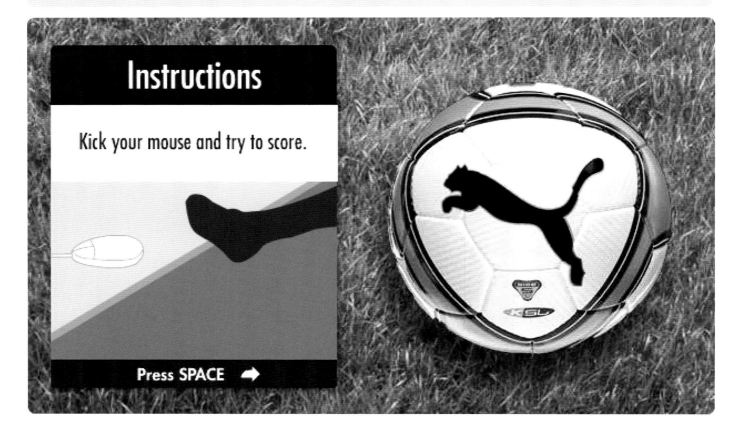

JUDGES' CHOICE

Project Rebirth Web Site . CLIENT // Project Rebirth
ANNUAL ID // 05237N

CHRISTOPHER FRANZESE
hanft raboy and partners/New York

Project Rebirth captured my interest immediately with its compelling content. Quickly, it became apparent that the site also demonstrates technical sophistication and an elegantly simple concept that, in spirit and technique, explores the history of our future.

Beginning six months after the attacks, time-lapse cameras positioned around Ground Zero continue to document the passage of ten years time. There is rich information in the form of photo galleries, interviews and journals from those involved with the rebuilding effort, but the content in the spotlight is the video timeline. An intuitive interface allows users to display video from the various cameras for variable durations. In so doing, the site explores the presentation of infinite, possible cuts of a video library.

With the growth of video databases, whether through omnipresent corporate and governmental cameras, through the sharing of personal experiences on video blogs and aggregators like Vimeo and Mefeedia, or through the foresight of documentarians like those at Project Rebirth, the opportunities for designers to create assisted and automated curatorial tools is going to enable a new way to collectively remember our generation.

JUDGES' CHOICE

Aiwaworld . CLIENT // Aiwa + ANNUAL ID // 05022N

SEAN PATRICK GANANN

NetX/Balmain, Australia

Surprising and immersive, vibrant, lively and lots of fun—the Aiwaworld site is my top choice from this year's One Show Interactive entries.

This is work that makes exceptional use of the medium, leveraging excellent sound design and charming illustration to create a surreal but creative environment. Within the environment, the audience is engaged to interact, explore and construct their own brand experience—guided of course by interestingly strange "aiwamals." It's an experience that is at once youthful and clearly audiovisual—reinforcing Aiwa's positioning.

JUDGES' CHOICE
AGENCY // Crispin Porter + Bogusky

CHRISTIAN HASS
Organic/San Francisco

It could have been revenge. But this time, the Web took central stage in some of the most memorable advertising campaigns of the year. They became synonymous with innovation and the subject of conversations, envy and inspiration among clients and agencies across the globe. How many times have you heard—or said to yourself, "I want to do the next Subservient Chicken?"

My favorite entry this year goes not just to the Chicken but to all of its side dishes: the amazing work of Crispin Porter + Bogusky. Work that dares to go beyond brand guidelines, yet is impeccably branded. Work that is never about the medium or the technology but is always about the idea. Work that the only gratuitous thing about it is the millions of people that passed it along. Work we can say is "above the online."

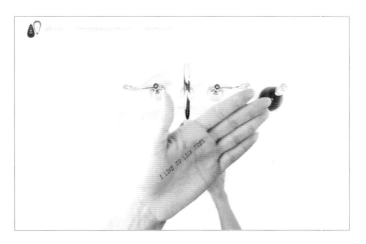

(above)
Crispin Porter + Bogusky
CLIENT // Method
ANNUAL ID // 05147N

(left)
Crispin Porter + Bogusky
CLIENT // Virgin
ANNUAL ID // 05006N

(right)
Crispin Porter + Bogusky
CLIENT // MINI USA
ANNUAL ID // 05091N

JUDGES' CHOICE

It's Time for JUBES . CLIENT // Wong Coco + ANNUAL ID // 05154N

NATHAN HACKSTOCK
TEQUILA\Los Angeles

For its ability to take something as unexceptional as a chewy translucent cube...

...and create an environment that entertains its visitors through a series
of engaging subtleties.

With a drag+drop+toss navigation, beady little cursor following eyes, random invites
to spread the word and time-delayed screen evolutions...

...I found myself learning more about this high-fiber, low-calorie, preservative and
cholesterol-free dessert than I ever thought possible.

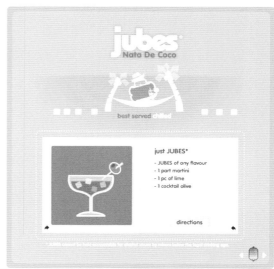

JUDGES' CHOICE
Silent Movie . CLIENT // 2001 Videolocadora + ANNUAL ID // 05019N

ROB HUDAK
New York

Though it may not be the most explosive, in-your-face promotion, this entry plays with the idea of interactivity and employs the kind of thinking that I appreciate in our medium. It exposes the mechanics of animation while exposing the mechanics of the computer and makes for what seems like a more physical interactivity when it is really not much more than the same click of a button. It succeeds in giving the illusion of a hand-cranked animation. Its somewhat clunky and tedious interaction turns the computer into a mechanical instrument and shows how the penny arcade and early film led us to where we are now.

JUDGES' CHOICE

Pet Sematary . CLIENT // NOAH Menschen für Tiere e. V. + ANNUAL ID // 05050N

MAYA KOPYTMAN
IconNicholson/New York

The entry that remained engraved in my mind was Pet Sematary, an interactive memorial for animals lost to the fur industry. About ten years ago a friend of mine approached me with a revolutionary idea. "Let's build a virtual cemetery on the Web!" he said. Well, just a reminder: dial-up, 256 colors, 640 x 480 resolution, what else? Flash? Who said Flash? Ten years later, when I happened to encounter Pet Sematary, all I could say was: "How come I didn't think about it?"

What is so brilliant about this site is how simple it is—you light a candle, write an obituary and read a fact or two about the fur industry. The message is quiet and understated, yet so overwhelmingly powerful. The design is equally moving in its minimalism. Seeing myself among thousands of protesters around the world made me realize again what a powerful medium the Web is today.

JUDGES' CHOICE

ConQwest Urban Geo Game . CLIENT // Qwest + ANNUAL ID // 05034N

SASHA KURTZ
Dotglu/New York

There were a lot of great entries this year, but my personal favorite was SS+K's ConQwest Urban Geo Game.

Half treasure hunt, half race, ConQwest was a truly mixed media event. Teams of high school students in five cities around the U.S. scoured the streets in search of "semacodes" which, when photographed by their Qwest-loaded Nokia phones, unlocked secret messages, points and clues to win the game. And, winning the game ultimately required moving enormous, inflatable, animal-shaped totems around the city.

Unfortunately, the photographs of this project don't really capture its many layers. Not only was it an immersive and fun game, it cut through the advertising clutter to engage a skeptical, savvy audience. Additionally, there was a single, unified, integrated message across multiple touch points—print, outdoor, interactive and PR. But most importantly, the creators never lost sight of the ultimate objective: to design an experience that would be exciting, and at the same time, highlight the technology of the product.

ROBERT RASMUSSEN
Wieden + Kennedy/Portland

I feel it was the freshest execution of 2004. It was truly interactive. SS+K addressed a clear target consumer—teenagers who use cell phones. They then created something that utilized these cell phones, as well as the Internet. The effect was something the target wanted to be a part of. And in huge numbers. This caught the attention of the media, who in turn covered the events.

Plus, it helped sell a lot of phones.

JUDGES' CHOICE

Dr. Angus . CLIENT // Burger King + ANNUAL ID // 05030N

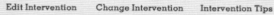

Edit Intervention   Change Intervention   Intervention Tips

> back to angusdiet.com

DR. ANGUS INTERVENTIONS

ED ROBINSON
Viral Factory/London

Crispin Porter + Bogusky's follow up to Subservient Chicken, the Dr. Angus campaign, was my pick of the competition, and not just because it features an iconic English comedian. I understand why many of my colleagues would argue that Subservient Chicken is a more groundbreaking campaign, and they probably have a point, but while Subservient Chicken helped define a medium (viral), Dr. Angus shows us how this channel should be used. It puts at the very heart of a campaign the concept of entertaining your audience first and foremost. The TV ads, the site, the downloadable book, and best of all, the Dr. Angus interventions all extend a great central idea with consistent quality and imagination. Most advertisers forget that online you're competing with three billion Web pages (and most of them aren't trying to sell you stuff and often want to show you things that frankly you're curious to see). So to attract an audience and keep them you have to do more than show them pictures of your products and headquarters. Crispin Porter + Bogusky understands this and as a result produces work as good and engaging as Dr. Angus. I'm jealous.

MICHAEL KUTSCHINSKI
OgilvyInteractive/Frankfurt

"Waaayyyytagoooo!!!"

No, it's not a new diet, but a brilliant Integrated Branding campaign. Dr. Angus is based on a simple idea with a perfect character as an actor, nice artwork and terrific copywriting. It acts like an oily antidote to the plethora of fad diets currently gripping the average consumer, those that urge you to eat healthily. You can see it, hear it and also take it away from the digital medium, because there is also a book to read. It gets you going, giving you the feeling that you need to eat a big, fat, juicy burger right now. "Do a nice workout for your abdominal muscles and read the Angus Diet book. You'll lose weight." That is what I told my friends by sending the viral part of the Web site all over the world. So it is a real diet.

In total not every single part of the campaign uses media in a brilliant way. The Web site is not a site which includes interactivity and the TV commercials are matter of taste. But all together it works very well.

The Integrated Branding campaign category is for me as an advertiser the most important category, because it shows a lot of different touch points to the consumer. This year, for me, Burger King broke the norm with every submission they entered in this category.

The world on the outside has changed.

Let us go on. It is the "Waaayyyytagoooo."

DR. ANGUS
• Enjoy *all* that life has to offer!
• Instant results.
• It's new!

AS SEEN ON TV

Eating the **ANGUS DIET**

Be more than full.
Be **FULFILLED!**

JUDGES' CHOICE

Nike ID . CLIENT // Nike + ANNUAL ID // 05181N

ERNEST LUPINACCI
Anomaly/New York

I'm a staunch proponent of the idea that here in the 21st century, the best ad for your brand is a great product. A good example of this is the Apple iPod—not the Apple iPod commercials—but the iPod itself, which, as my good pal Jim Surowewiecki put it in an article for *Wired* magazine, "...did more for Apple, than Apple did for the iPod."

Enter the Nike ID Web site, literally and figuratively.

Here is an opportunity for the consumer to revel in the brand on the product level, and experience it in the most individual and iconoclastic way. Talk about bringing "Just Do It" to life. Every pair is unique, every pair is a piece of advertising, every pair is a brand extension, and not to be crass, but every pair is another pair sold.

To the credit of the folks at R/GA, they took a fantastic product innovation—Nike figuring out mass-customization—and built a Web site that over-delivered on it.

Orson Welles was famous for saying, "Don't give 'em what they want, give 'em what they didn't even think they could have..." My hats off to Nike and R/GA for giving me what I didn't even think I could have.

JUDGES' CHOICE

Red Bull Co-pilot . CLIENT // Red Bull + ANNUAL ID // 05157N

SIMON MILLISHIP
Wunderman Interactive/London

When you pitch an idea for a site, and the client buys it, it is rare that the finished product matches the original concept once the site goes live.

Red Bull Co-Pilot strikes me as one of those great ideas that made it through the entire creative and production roller coaster and survived intact. The site just oozes killer code delivered successfully online. The experience is immersive, interactive and resonates the Red Bull brand to the max.

The execution is spot on and cleverly delivers a racing experience that exploits original footage shot from the multiple angles a viewer would choose to see during a race.

Being able to switch views in real time to experience the race in intense detail is fantastic and the commentary brings the whole thing to life.

For my money, Red Bull Co-Pilot does what it says on the tir ...

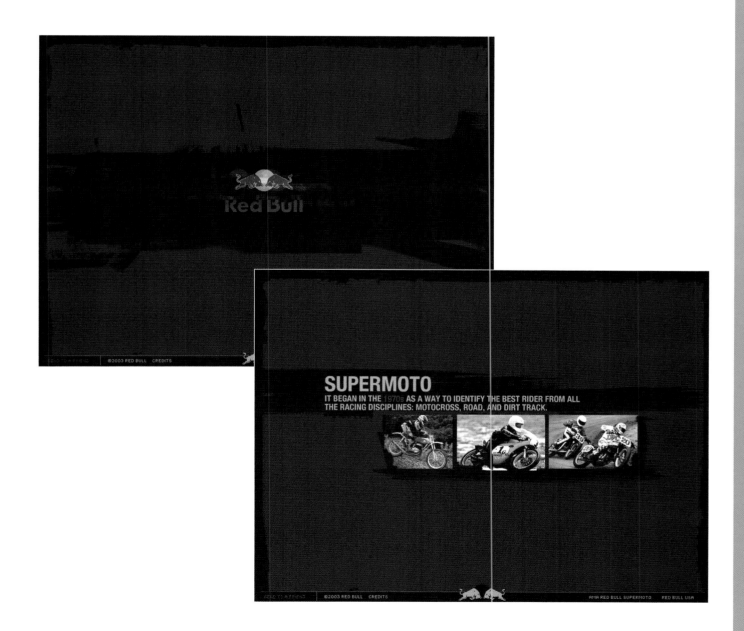

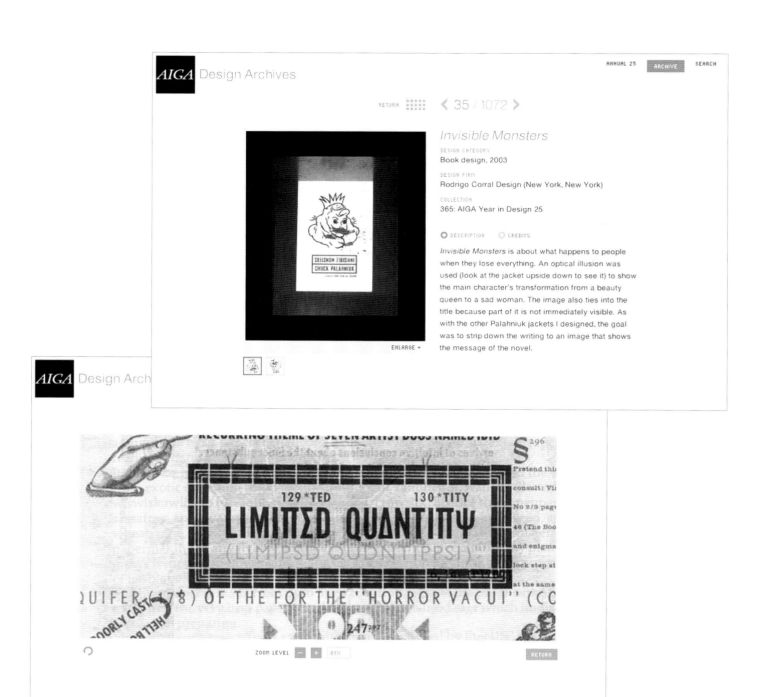

JUDGES' CHOICE

AIGA Design Archive . CLIENT // AIGA + ANNUAL ID // 05051N

TOKE NYGAARD
Cuban Council/New York

It is useful, clear and very well-executed. Going through hundreds of entries, this one really stuck with me.

Functionality like the Lightbox and the ability to zoom in on all the archived material works well, and the whole package has that professional and airy feel that I would expect from AIGA—though it still retains that informal playfulness that makes me want to dive right into it.

JUDGES' CHOICE

Jump in Game . CLIENT // MINI USA + ANNUAL ID // 05042N

NAOTO OIWA
Dentsu/Tokyo

Even though you fail in launching yourself into the MINI and only end up hurting yourself and making dents in the car, the brand image of MINI doesn't get any damage at all. This is because I think the idea and the way of presenting this convertible is just incredible!

JUDGES' CHOICE
Hope . CLIENT // GRAACC + ANNUAL ID // 05053N

MATIAS PALM-JENSEN
Farfar/Stockholm

There's a trend in the industry today I don't like at all: The respect for the audience is lacking. The traditional ad industry tries to squeeze in their regular spots on the Web. They fail to respect the Internet user and they don't realize the possibilities of using film in a more creative and interactive way.

We have to remember that in our business we don't buy time—we have to create time. And I'm not talking about magical tricks or being too clever. Try to resist donating money after interacting in the beautiful "haiku-made" piece, Hope for GRAACC.

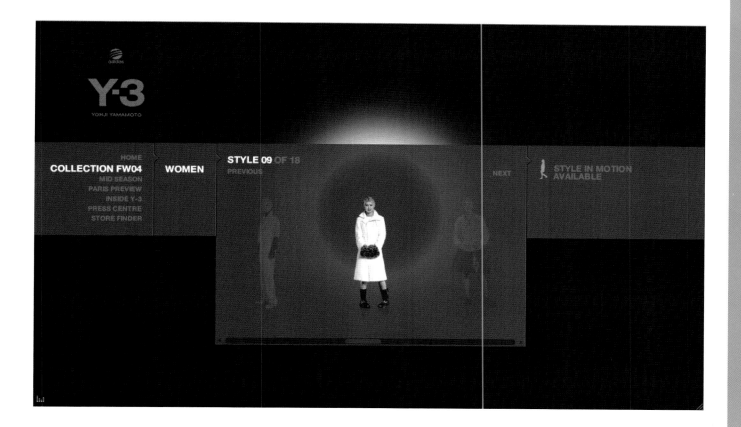

JUDGES' CHOICE

adidas Sport Style Y-3 . CLIENT // adidas-Salomon AG + ANNUAL ID // 05021N

TOM ROOPE
tomato/London

For me the piece that gave me the greatest "wish I had done that" was the Y-3 Web site. You could get a sense of the attention to details, and utter passion that must have been part of the production. The live action shoot was one of the best I have seen online, and it was almost impossible to see the beautifully crafted loops, and I particularly liked the reflection that was comped in where the treadmill matted out. It was also how technical aspects such as asset loading were dealt with in a holistic and fluid manner. The interface approach was also open and exploratory.

I have worked with on-screen fashion for several years and this piece was head and shoulders above any I have seen in its sector. It was really nice to see a piece of work that was about beauty and elegance, after seeing reams of sites that are smart-arsed one liners.

BRIGITTE VON PUTTKAMER
Framfab/Munich

One of my favorite entries is adidas Sport Style Y-3 created by Neue Digitale, Frankfurt, presenting the autumn/winter 2004 Y-3 collection. Having studied fashion design myself I really like the way clothing is presented on this trend-setting Web site.

Watching streamed videos of walking models, the user can not only see the color, the pattern and the cut, but also grasp the character of the fabric, its weave and weight. This really is an achievement, getting a decisive step closer to a real online shopping spree.

Take a look at the technical aspects: no nerve-wracking loading sequences here, which tend to interrupt the emotional pull of animated Web sites. A very good piece of work indeed!

JUDGES' CHOICE
Subservient Chicken . CLIENT // Burger King + ANNUAL ID // 05020N

NIK ROOPE
Poke/London

I'm going to pick Subservient Chicken. Hardly a controversial choice. In fact, even as I wrote the words down I became a part of a worldwide cult of Subservient Chicken worshippers, award judges who struggled to find anything more compelling in the cream of our industry's output.

Subservient Chicken is good. It's funny. It isn't, however, that innovative or groundbreaking.

The reason I have picked this is that the project is a triumph of risk-taking on both agency and client side. It demonstrates to the world that ideas and humor, not obsessive production values, and safe but predictable media buying are driving interest on the Web. This is good creative thinking engineered to create huge, tangible value.

Too often, "creativity" and the "idea" are considered something confined to creative departments. But real progressive work is defined as much through clients being prepared to take the leap as it is strong, willful creative direction. Subservient Chicken as a case study predicts a fundamental shift in the way we need to approach interactive advertising, an approach that requires a new way of working and thinking.

This project is already redefining the agenda. If these awards are about setting industry benchmarks for all to learn from then Subservient Chicken should be up there.

JUDGES' CHOICE

The Germanwings Realtime Screensaver
CLIENT // Germanwings + ANNUAL ID // 05025N

PAULO SANNA
OgilvyInteractive/New York

My favorite entry from this year's One Show Interactive was the screen saver—or rather, the desktop application—that Neue Digitale did for Germanwings. The idea of providing Internet users with real time information about the actual position of each aircraft is just too smart.

To me, it was one of those rare opportunities when everything was there at the same time: a very nice idea, a beautiful execution, a relevant offer and a perfect use of the interactive space. Everything done with extreme simplicity, from the technology behind the application to the interface design. I wish I had had this idea.

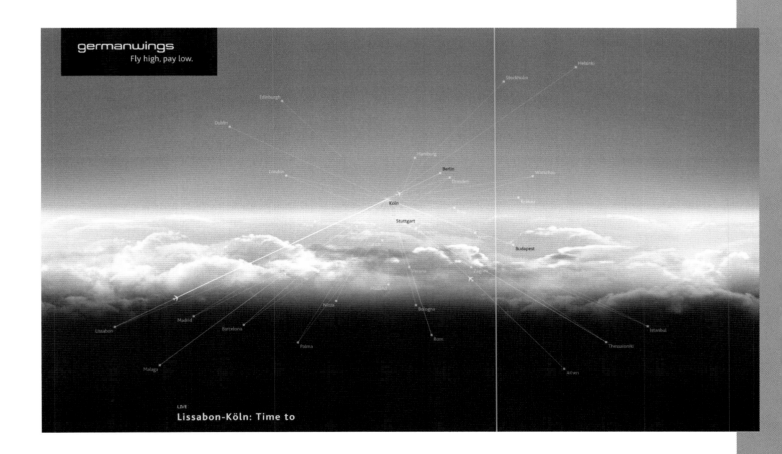

JUDGES' CHOICE

Saw . CLIENT // Lion Gate Films, USA + ANNUAL ID // 05015N

MICHAEL VOLKMER
Scholz & Volkmer/Wiesbaden

The Saw movie Web site, created by High-Res!, London, is almost as unbearably exciting as the movie itself. The design, picture language, typography, style methods, sound and audio reflect the character of the psycho horror movie perfectly without giving too much of the plot away.

The user is completely in the dark as he/she moves from one scene to the next, a problem solved in an impressive way by the explorative navigation, and forgets that he/she is actually sitting in front of a computer.

The movie's disturbed ideas have been transferred intelligently to the Web. Fast performance and high user integration through extensive interaction definitely creates an atmosphere that makes the user want to spend an above-average amount of time on the site.

Extraordinary!

JUDGES' CHOICE

Haircut . CLIENT // Virgin + ANNUAL ID // 05001N

STEVE VRANAKIS
VCCP/London

Forget everything they told you about click-throughs, view-throughs and etc., and start thinking "break-throughs." That's exactly what this Virgin Haircut ad unit is. It's got nothing to do with the quantity but everything to do with the quality of user interaction. Very much like the Virgin Upper Class experience itself.

Part of a fantastic campaign, including the Massage banner and the Dream interpreter, it sums up what Virgin Upper Class is all about. This execution epitomizes the notion of a positive brand experience. I messed around on it for a good few minutes.

Using a clever and well-branded technical illustration style, the viewer can upload their own picture into the ad unit live on a Web site and go to work on their hair. That's it.

Uploading locally stored images is by no means new, but it is the combination of relevance, simplicity and capturing the brand's tone of voice that makes this a "cutting edge" bit of creative. Although I would never condone the use of scissors on-board, especially while touching down at Hong Kong's old Kai Tak airport, but if this on-line experience is any sign of the Virgin on-board experience then this execution is in a class of its own.

Recognize anyone?

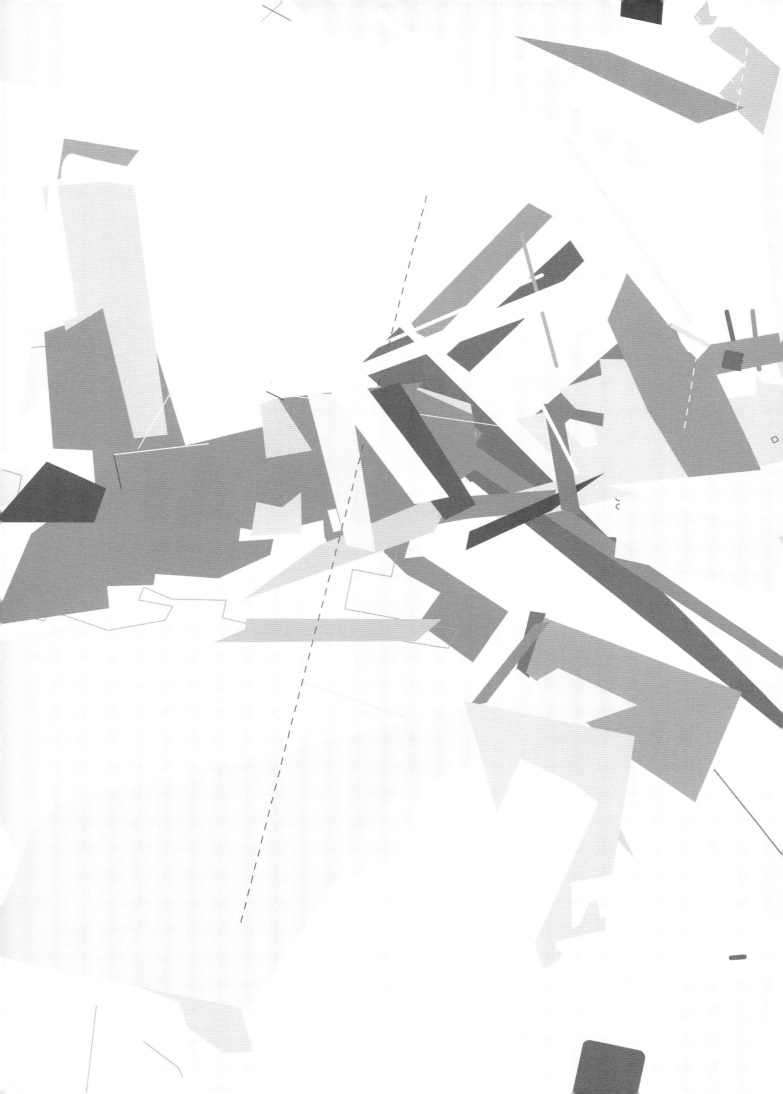

29 m95

CLIENT OF THE YEAR

BURGER KING
CLIENT OF THE YEAR

ANDY BONAPARTE
Senior Director, Advertising & Multicultural Marketing
Burger King Corporation

Burger King Corporation (BKC) is thrilled to receive the coveted One Show Interactive "Client of the Year." We believe that the interactive medium provides a unique platform to engage the consumer in our brand on a personal level. BKC is committed to creating unique and innovative brand experiences that surprise, entertain and excite our consumers while reinforcing our HAVE IT YOUR WAY® brand promise.

On behalf of BKC, I would like to thank our lead creative agency, Crispin Porter + Bogusky, for their award-winning contributions. With their help, we hope to continue to reinforce category thought leadership by redefining the boundaries of online marketing.

Agency
Crispin Porter + Bogusky/Miami
Annual ID
05032N

Eating the **ANGUS DIET**

Eating the **ANGUS DIET**

Agency
Crispin Porter + Bogusky/Miami
Annual ID
05030N (above), 05096N (below)

Agency
Crispin Porter + Bogusky/Miami
Annual ID
05095N

Agency
Crispin Porter + Bogusky/Miami
Annual ID
05149N

BK Salads

"Please... I'm Ugoff. I can design a pouch with my eyes closed. If I had my hands tied behind my back, I could design a pouch with my toes."

Apple Orchard Wrist Clutch	Half Moon Silver Clutch	The Pouch
Rafe New York, $115	*Sigerson Morrison*, $310	BURGER KING,
www.rafe.com	www.sigersonmorrison.com	$4.39 Shrimp/ $3.99 Chicken
		www.bk.com
		*price and participation may vary.

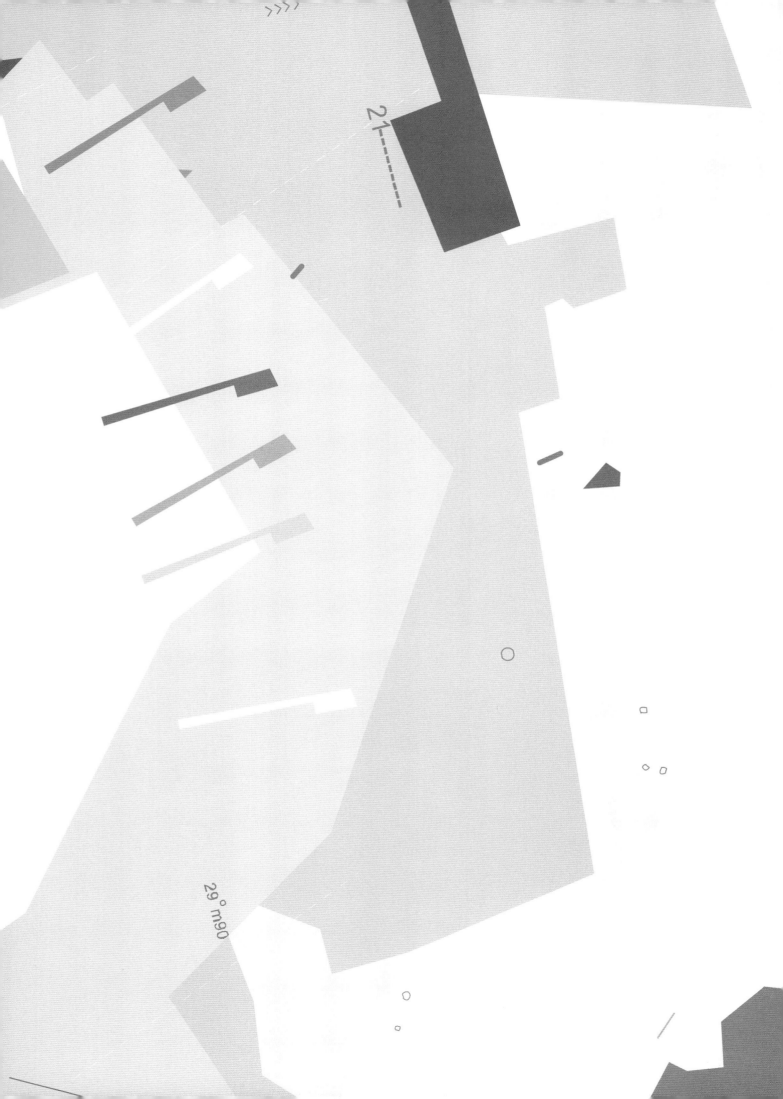

21

29° m90

BEST OF SHOW

DANCE, CHICKEN, DANCE!

Putting a completely unique spin on Burger King's tried and true "Have it Your Way" tagline, Crispin Porter + Bogusky changed the Zeitgeist with Subservient Chicken, a giant chicken that does exactly what it's told. Building off the TV campaign's success, the Subservient Chicken webcam became a bona fide phenomenon and redefined interactive advertising.

Agency
Crispin Porter + Bogusky/
Miami
Client
Burger King
Art Director
Mark Taylor
Writer
Bob Cianfrone
Illustrator
Pres Rodriguez
Agency Producers
David Rolfe, Terry Stavoe
Production Companies
MJZ, The Barbarian Group

Information Architects
Mutato Muzika (music),
Beacon Street (music)
Director
Rocky Morton
Creative Directors
Alex Bogusky, Andrew Keller,
Jeff Benjamin, Rob Reilly
Annual ID
05031N
URL
www.cpbgroup.com/awards/
subservient_int.html
Also Awarded
Gold Award:
Corporate Image B2C . Web Sites

There is a reason this site captured Best of Show. The concept seems very rooted in the classic Burger King "Have It Your Way" brand message. Can you talk about the development of the site and the larger "Have It Your Way" framework?
Well, the assignment was pretty straightforward. Introduce Burger King's new TenderCrisp Chicken Sandwich under the "Have It Your Way" brand platform. We came up with a TV campaign based on a large bird that did exactly what it was told. People tell it to dance, or put on a vest or pick up something off the ground. And the bird just follows orders. We called it Subservient Chicken. It drove the brand message home pretty well. We then started thinking about a Web component, and came up with the idea of having Subservient Chicken in a webcam. To let people have chicken just the way they like it, on an even larger scale. We spent a day filming Subservient Chicken performing commands. We put it all together with keywords attached and launched the site.

Practically overnight, the site was a phenomenon. Was anyone prepared for its success?
Not really. We all thought it was a cool idea. We had people in the office test the Beta version out, and they all seemed to like it. So we assumed there would be some interest. But no one expected the response we got.

Given the progressive nature of the site, was it a difficult concept to sell to Burger King?
No. Burger King was great. They embraced it right away. They know who they are talking to. They know they have to communicate in new and interesting ways. They were supportive all the way through.

 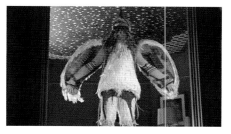

07° j4

PENCIL WINNERS

FOREST
PRESERVATION FINDS
ITS PERFECT MEDIUM

Despite it being a banner in a sea of cyberspace, the attention-grabbing
message stands out: paper comes from trees and by extension, wasted
paper represents wasted forest. Hakuhodo's smooth motion Flash execution
commands attention, highlighting the grave message.

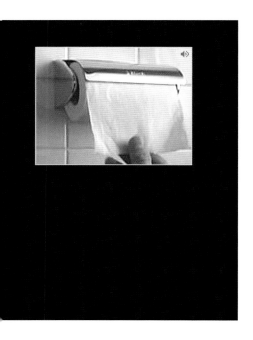

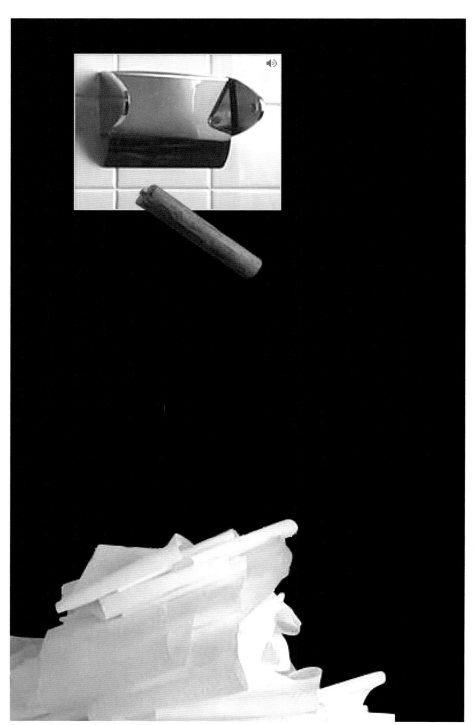

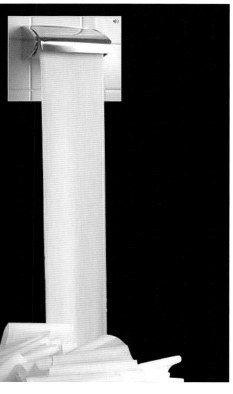

SAVE PAPER
SAVE FOREST

WWF

Agency
Hakuhodo/Tokyo
Client
World Wide Fund for Nature Japan
Art Directors
Yohei Ishida, Yukio Sato
Writer
Toshiya Fukuda
Digital Artist/Multimedia
Yukio Sato
Production Companies
TYO Interactive Design, 777 Interactive
Programmer
Tomoyuki Tada
Designers
Yukio Sato, Shuhei Umene
Creative Directors
Toshiya Fukuda, Takayoshi Kishimoto
URL
http://www.tyo-id.co.jp/works/
banner/2004/wwf/02.html
Annual ID
05002N

Describe the brief from the client and your creative approach.
As you see in our daily life, Japan is a major consumer of paper. In the cycle of global
economy, this consumption causes trees in Asia to be cut down and animals to loose
their place to live. We wanted to make an ad that makes people aware of this issue.

What was the concept of these banners?
Instead of denying the use of paper completely, we wanted to focus on the message:
Wasteful, excessive use of paper destroys nature. We decided to use a simple expression
to let people realize that their daily habit has influence on a global issue.

How did you approach the execution?
Since ordinary objects and habits were the subject of this message, we especially
put effort in depicting the realness. We mainly used Flash and skipped frames to create
smooth movement as the user operates with a mouse.

GOLD

OVERWRAPPED POLITENESS

A simple banner brings into question the virtually unquestioned etiquette of gift wrapping. More to the point, the banner underscores the problem of excessive paper waste. Hakuhodo achieved the Matryoshka doll-like executions utilizing Flash technology.

 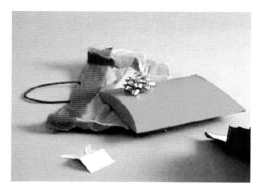

Agency
Hakuhodo/Tokyo
Client
World Wide Fund for Nature Japan
Art Directors
Miwako Nishikawa, Yasuo Nihei
Writer
Toshiya Fukuda
Digital Artist/Multimedia
Yasuo Nihei
Production Companies
TYO Interactive Design,
777 Interactive
Designers
Yasuo Nihei, Shuhei Umene
Creative Directors
Toshiya Fukuda,
Takayoshi Kishimoto
URL
http://www.tyo-id.co.jp/works/
banner/2004/wwf/03.html
Annual ID
05003N

SAVE PAPER
SAVE FOREST

A VERY CHEEKY E-CARD

Ever dreamed of writing a message with a tattoo gun on someone's butt and sending it to a friend or collegue? Elephant Seven makes that fantasy a reality and at the same time captures the irreverent car culture of Motoraver Magazine with a naughty e-card.

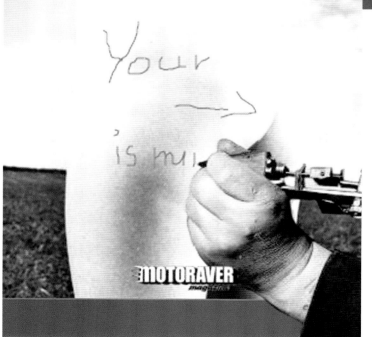

Agency
Elephant Seven GmbH Nord/
Hamburg
Client
Motoraver Verlag
Art Director
Sven Giese
Writer
Florian Matthies
Programmer
Kim Christiansen
Information Architect
Rainer Sax
Creative Director
Oliver Viets
URL
http://bannertool.e-7.com/
awards/arschgeweih/
Annual ID
05004N

HIEROGLYPHICS
MADE EASY

Utilizing Flash animation to visualize words, OgilvyInteractive demonstrates that learning a language is all about association for CNA-English School*.

*CNA is an English School whose methodology offers a direct connection to the students' real life. So, the campaign introduces simple English lessons, showing how you can learn easily and naturally while having a moment of fun.

When you realize it, you´re already talking. | CNA English School

When you realize it, you´re already talking. | CNA English School

MouSe

MouSe

C

cat

DOG

cat

DOG

LiOn

elephant

MouSe

English School | **When you realize it,
you´re already talking.** MouSe

Agency
OgilvyInteractive/São Paulo
Client
CNA - English School
Art Director
Pedro Gravena
Writer
Miguel Genovese
Content Strategist
Patricia Weiss
Creative Directors
Marco Antônio de Almeida,
Paulo Sanna, Adriana Cury
URL
www.ourwork.com.br/subtitles
Annual ID
05005N

GOLD

BANNER UPGRADE

Crispin Porter + Bogusky further establishes Virgin Atlantic Airway's Upper Class experience as both a uniquely fun and relaxing way to fly. In a series of seductive and witty executions inspired by airplane emergency instruction art, the banners are a clear break from traditional airline advertising.

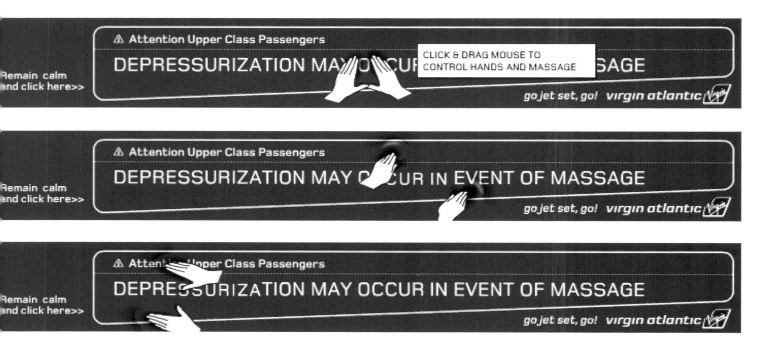

Agency
Crispin Porter + Bogusky/Miami
Client
Virgin
Art Directors
Juan-Carlos Morales,
Michael Ferrare
Writers
Franklin Tipton, Dustin Ballard,
David Gonzalez, Justin Kramm
Production Companies
Milky Elephant,
The Barbarian Group
Creative Directors
Alex Bogusky, Bill Wright,
Andrew Keller, Jeff Benjamin
URL
www.cpbgroup.com/awards/
bannersAoneshow.html
Annual ID
05006N

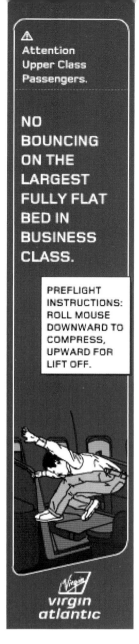

Also Awarded
(bottom left)
Gold Award: Banners . Single

(top left and right)
Merit Awards: Banners . Single

JOB PLACEMENT
FOR "FUN"

Conceptually rooted in savvy media placement, OgilvyInteractive develops a series of quirky banners that directly equate Sony PlayStation with the very notion of "fun."

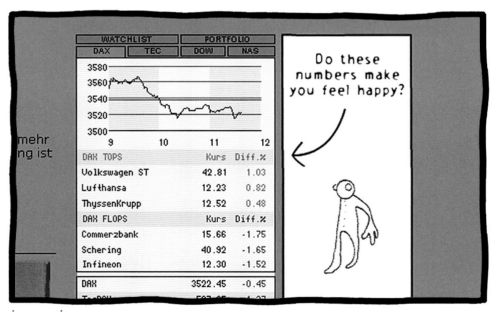

Agency
OgilvyInteractive/
Frankfurt am Main
Client
PlayStation
Art Director
Thorsten Voigt
Writer
Andrea Goebel
Designer
Thorsten Voigt
Information Architect
Andrea Goebel
Creative Director
Michael Kutschinski
URL
http://www.ourwork.de/
oneshow/playstation/banner
Annual ID
05007N

What challenges did you face in creating the banner-specific hosting sites?
The main target was to create a seamless integration with the banner and the Web site
itself. Lengthy discussions with our media agency enabled us to conjure up a special
and individual way to do this. Lycos loved the ideas and after discussions about technical
barriers, it was brought to life. For example, the PlayStation bird on the Lycos site is seen
stealing one of the navigation buttons, where the slogan "fun, anyone?" is revealed.

How did the team come up with the "fun, anyone?" slogan?
The slogan "fun, anyone?" is part of the worldwide positioning of PlayStation. We wanted
to interpret the slogan in a new way for the Internet, keeping in mind at all times two
specific points: First, let's bring "fun" to the Web; second, target specific Web sites due to
target group preferences, then tailor interactivity and animation to suit them.

What were the technical challenges in creating the animation?
Keeping the file size down to a bare minimum was the main challenge. To achieve this we
just used a very specific part of the original animation. For example, Robogirl is based on
four different pictures. The hard one was to give an impression of slick motion graphics
with a limited number of frames. Luckily due to the quirkiness of the idea, the slightly jerky
movements actually added a special quality to the final animation.

STREET SIGN
ESCAPISM

Various street signs fluidly morphing into recreational signs
by Fallon communicate the tagline "Escape From Everyday Life"
for The Islands Of The Bahamas Ministry Of Tourism.

Agency
Fallon/Minneapolis
Client
The Islands Of The Bahamas
Ministry Of Tourism
Art Director
Nathan Hinz
Writer
Russ Stark
Digital Artists/Multimedia
Chris Stocksmith, Laurie Brown,
Tal Tahir, Tony Litner
Programmers
Chris Stocksmith, Laurie Brown,
Tal Tahir, Tony Litner
Designers
Nathan Hinz, Chris Stocksmith
Creative Directors
Kevin Flatt, Todd Riddle
URL
http://awards.fallon.com/
index.aspx?pro=201
Annual ID
05009N

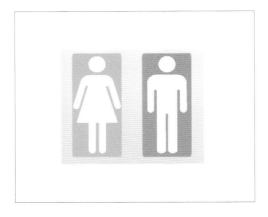

Can you talk about the challenge of getting people's attention and generating awareness while remaining true to the "Escape From Everyday Life" platform?

The "Escape From Everyday Life" campaign contrasts common, everyday reminders of our day-in and day-out drudgery with the natural beauty and multiplicity of The Islands Of The Bahamas. The challenge was to translate that idea into a breakthrough, compelling online campaign that drives traffic to bahamas.com. The "Signs" campaign specifically focuses on various information signs that one might see daily. The campaign transformed these everyday signs into something more interesting and exciting that's available in the Bahamas—like a crosswalk sign into a scuba diver, an escalator into a waterslide, and a deer crossing into a dolphin sighting. The animations transform the expected into the unexpected, giving you a signal that it's time to "Escape From Everyday Life" to The Islands Of The Bahamas.

The animation is very fluid. Were there technical obstacles in achieving the effect?

One of the reasons we chose to extend the "Escape From Everyday Life" campaign in this way is that the graphic nature of signs lent itself to flash well, allowing us to create very real-looking signs out of vector-based art. Once we had determined which sign was going to turn into what Bahamian activity, we put a lot of effort into keeping all the parts as simple as possible, and let the big impact come from the animation and timing. Part of the fluidity of the banners is the result of a lot of activity happening in less than a second. We paid special attention to the speed a canoe might slow down after an oar stroke, how a dolphin wiggles back and forth as it swims backwards, or the different poses a person makes during a dive. We felt it was important that they feel more like animated spots than typical banners, but still work in under 8 seconds from beginning to end.

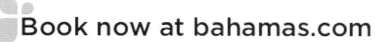

HEWLETT-PACKARD DOES KANDINSKY

Through a series of abstract animations, Goodby, Silverstein & Partners interprets different musical genres visually, introducing the Apple iPod from HP while maintaining the long-established Hewlett-Packard aesthetic.

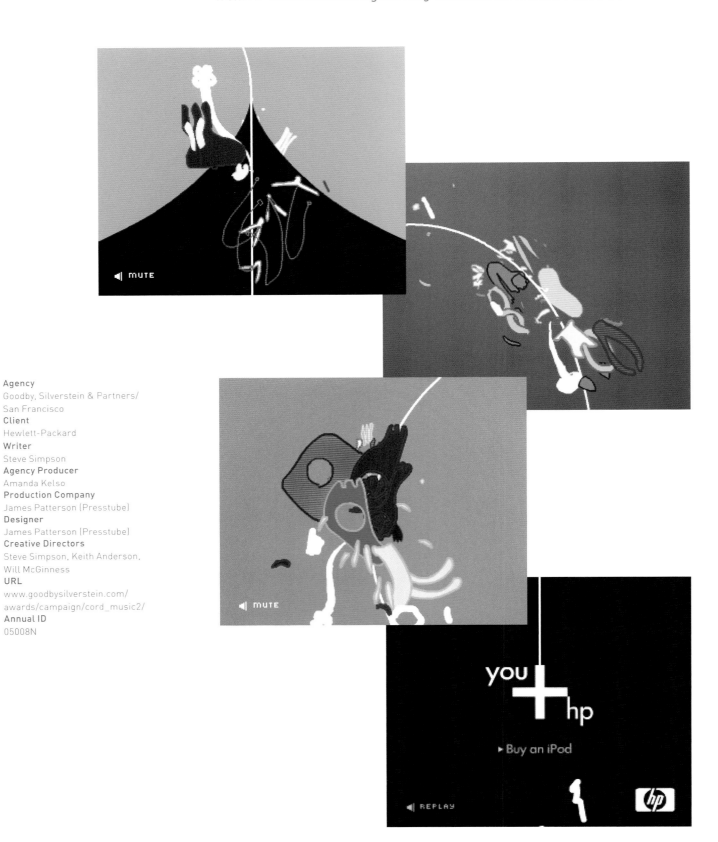

Agency
Goodby, Silverstein & Partners/
San Francisco
Client
Hewlett-Packard
Writer
Steve Simpson
Agency Producer
Amanda Kelso
Production Company
James Patterson (Presstube)
Designer
James Patterson (Presstube)
Creative Directors
Steve Simpson, Keith Anderson,
Will McGinness
URL
www.goodbysilverstein.com/
awards/campaign/cord_music2/
Annual ID
05008N

The ads visually represent the frenetic energy of music.
What was your approach of translating music into an animated banner?
The main challenge was to create a distinct identity for Hewlett-Packard's entry into digital music with its introduction of the Apple iPod from HP. The campaign sought to highlight that experience of playing music on a portable digital music player by mixing organic imagery with a diverse range of music, from Rock to World to Hip Hop, which visually represents each listener's musical world.

Was there an animator or style you had in mind
or did the style develop during the creative process?
When we started the campaign, we followed the theme that listening to music is not passive, but rather, an active form of personal expression. We were drawn to the work of James Patterson of Presstube, whose animation style is flowing and lyrical. In our collaboration with James, we were able to explore that concept of listening to music as an active and creative experience.

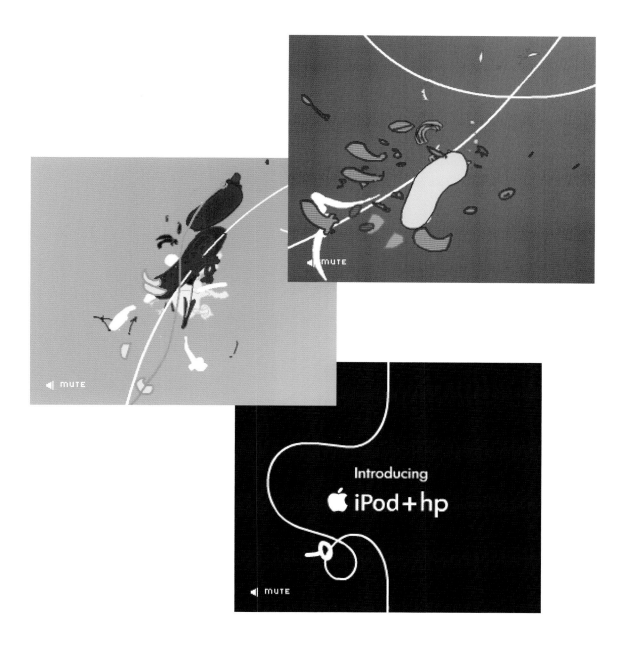

GLEAMING THE STORE

Faced with public perception of überhipness, JC Clothes sought to reclaim all strata of consumers. For the web site, Forsman & Bodenfors creates a mosaic to visualize the sexiness and democratic appeal of JC Clothes.

THE SURVIVORS WEARS 470 ELEKTRA
REPLAY. JEANS WITH LOW WAIST AND
STRAIGHT LEG. BUTTON FLY. (FEMALE) SEK
FROM 999 NOK FROM 1199. AND CROCKER
355 C70 VB-VINTAGE. JEANS WITH NORMAL
TILTED WAIST. STRAIGHT FIT AND WITH
COMFORT BOOTCUT. BUTTON FLY.
(MALE/UNISEX). SEK/NOK 699 , EURO 79,90

THE COMMERCIALS
FIND A STORE
TIP A FRIEND
CONTACT
SOUND

Agency
Forsman & Bodenfors/
Gothenburg
Client
JC Clothes
Art Directors
Andreas Malm,
Mathias Appelblad
Writer
Fredrik Jansson
Digital Artist/Multimedia
Kokokaka Entertainment
Designer
Jerry Wass
URL
http://demo.fb.se/
e/jc/thestore
Annual ID
05011N

What was the brief for the "Store" section of JC?
JC is a clothing-store chain that for several years worked on being as young and hip
as possible, just as clothing-store chains are expected to act. And they succeeded.
For every year that passed, the target group became younger and younger and hipper
and hipper. In the end, there was only a tiny, tiny bunch of customers who were as young
and hip as was needed to shop at JC. And the shops began to look alarmingly empty.

The brief was clear: win back customers who had been scared away. Tell them that JC
had clothes, especially jeans, for everyone. No matter who you are: old or young, big
or small, boy or girl, cool or geeky. But do this without losing the sense of fashion.

This work successfully expands other forms of advertising media.
Was there any focal aspect the team paid attention to?
Integration across different medias. Since we took a completely new approach in JC's
advertising and abandoned the past, it was unusually important to have an absolutely
homogeneous tone, create a red thread and, at the same time, a feeling of a big change.
We also wanted, naturally, to use each media channel to the utmost.

When the commercial started being shown on TV, we released the specially made music
on this campaign Web site, where visitors also could see the commercial and check
out all the types of jeans that were in the commercial. The print campaign recreated the
feeling in the commercial, as did all the material in the shops

Was there a problem implementing the access from low-band users?
We always strive to make the experience as striking as possible. For this piece
we developed a very sophisticated loader. Even if you're watching it on a low-band
connection, you'll never experience the loading time for very long.

BUILDING A MYSTERY

With a highly dark and interactive narrative, Randommedia stirs a creepy Japanese urban legend with surprise and intrigue for PlayStation's "Forbidden Siren" game. The result is a memorable, multi-layered and yes, scary, interactive experience.

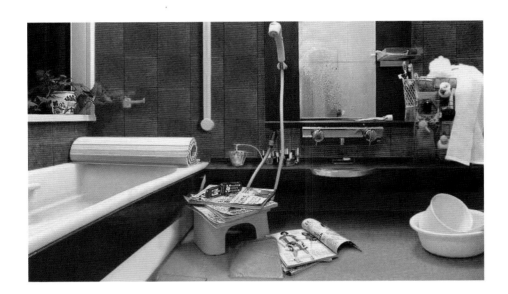

Agency
Randommedia/London
Client
Sony Computer
Entertainment Europe
Art Director
Duncan Bone
Designer
Xyn Xyu
URL
www.randommedia.
co.uk/siren
Annual ID
05012N

The navigation of the site is a game in and of itself so far as there is a sequence you must go through to reach the sneak preview of the game. How did this approach take form?
The original idea came from looking at many horror films: Everything seems normal at first, you get to know the characters from simple everyday events, then things start to go a bit weird, and then suddenly all hell breaks loose and you are thrown in the midst of brain-eating-zombies or chainsaw-wielding-maniacs or its equivalent. The site was built with the same format in mind.

It's not very good horror if everything happens the way you expect. With the site, when the user gets used to how the site works, there are surprises scattered about, like the chat window popping up, the phone ringing, downloads, etc. After all, exploring each room isn't routine.

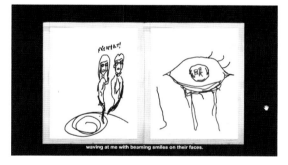

There are many layers of content to the site.

Was there an overarching vision from the beginning or did one idea fuel the next?

The content is actually quite basic, 4 rooms for 4 characters, with a few events in each room and a video sequence after the user sees all the events. After the user explores all 4 rooms, a final room/video sequence is released. We worked with this site structure in mind and beefed things up as we went along.

How difficult was the actual programming on par with other assignments?

The challenge was to optimize the video content and preloading cleverly, because the site was getting big in terms of file size. What we did was preload the expected content while the user is viewing certain sections of the site. So if the user actually sits down and goes through all the content, he/she shouldn't have to wait very long at all. We've done it since then for other sites like The Getaway: Black Monday, but as Siren was the first time we did this, it took a fair amount of experimenting with things like video compression and a combination of preloading and streaming to make sure that the site didn't get too heavy and that it works with different speeds.

A CAR TO BUILD
A DREAM ON

Goodby, Silverstein & Partners weaves a series of incongruous narratives that illuminate the myriad features of the Relay, a family-oriented SUV. The split-screen allows for a close and broad view, hinting at clues to discover.

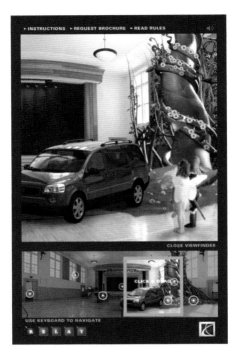

Agency
Goodby, Silverstein & Partners/
San Francisco
Client
Saturn
Art Director
Will McGinness
Writer
Aaron Griffiths
Agency Producer
Kenan Gregory
Production Company
North Kingdom
Creative Directors
Jamie Barrett, Keith Anderson,
Will McGinness
URL
www.goodbysilverstein.com/
awards/relay_minisite/
Annual ID
05013N

Can you talk about how you approached the design of the site while implementing the relevant Saturn content?
The idea of integrating information with experience was built into the concept. We wanted to make sure that as we were providing product info, we were doing it in an engaging and entertaining way. This also reflected Saturn's philosophy of no-haggle, no-hassle sales, allowing people to get what they want as they want it, not forcing it upon them.

There are some really nice rewards the users stumble upon. How important was it to reward them for taking time to surf the site?
The site does require time to fully experience, and we wanted to make sure that if users were willing to spend that time, we rewarded them for doing so. Once again, this aligned with the commitment to customer service that is a fundamental part of the Saturn brand.

THE NEED FOR SPEED

R/GA creates a minimalistic, economical, planetarium-like theater
for Nike Lab. The spaceship–inspired site houses 15 contemporary
artists' renderings of speed that further propel the Nike brand.

Agency
R/GA/New York
Client
Nike
Art Director
Jerome Austria
Writer
Jason Marks
Programmers
Kenric McDowell,
Lucas Shuman
Content Strategists
Jennifer Allen, Daniel Jurow
Designers
Gui Borchert, Mikhail Gervits,
Elena Sakevich, Hiroko Ishimura
Information Architect
Carlos Gomez de Llarena
URL
http://awards.web.rga.com/
2004/artofspeed.html
Annual ID
05014N

FRAGMENTING
A NIGHTMARE

Hi-ReS! was given the assignment of recreating the suspense and horror of the film "Saw" on the Web. Through bold graphics, jerky Flash animation and jarring audio, they translate the terror of the film while giving the site a life of its own.

Agency
Hi-ReS!/London
Client
Lions Gate Films, USA
Art Director
Florian Schmitt
Digital Artists/Multimedia
Florian Schmitt,
Tommi Eberwein, Marc Kremers
Programmers
Bela Spahn, Andreas Müller
Designer
Alexandra Jugovic
Creative Director
Alexandra Jugovic
URL
http://www.hi-res.net/
awards/saw
Annual ID
05015N

Can you describe the challenges of translating the passive act of film
watching to the engaging experience of interacting with the site?
We have a term for the technique we use on our sites: Assisted Discovery. It allows us
to employ a coherent narrative, without making the site necessarily a linear experience.
It's akin to what the Russian cinema called fabula, the act of mental chronological
reconstruction of the events of a non-chronological narrative. That may sound extremely
pretentious, but it's exactly what happens on our Web sites. We retain some control over
the sequence of events, however the path and the pace is controlled by you. It makes you
feel part of the narrative to a greater extent, which makes it intriguing.

How did you approach the challenge of maintaining the atmosphere
and tone the movie achieves through the site itself?
Music and sound. I think visually we had a pretty firm grip on things and in general we do
"dark and disturbed" very well, but in this case, the sound was very important—especially
as the killer is only identifiable by his voice.

Did the fact that the film is a suspense thriller suggest making
the site a suspenseful, interactive corollary game of sorts?
The whole film was a puzzle, which in itself was full of puzzles. The original plan was
to have a much more intense interactive game structure, but it was quickly getting too
complicated and would have diluted the experience. We settled for an approach which
would still let you discover, but was more straightforward and instantly rewarding.

OBEY YOUR INSTINCT

What do you get when you mix a Web site with a movie, a giant hamster in an animal experimentation lab, and human test subjects mixing a sound board? An advertisment for Sprite, obviously. Framfab Denmark goes for broke with hamster fun.

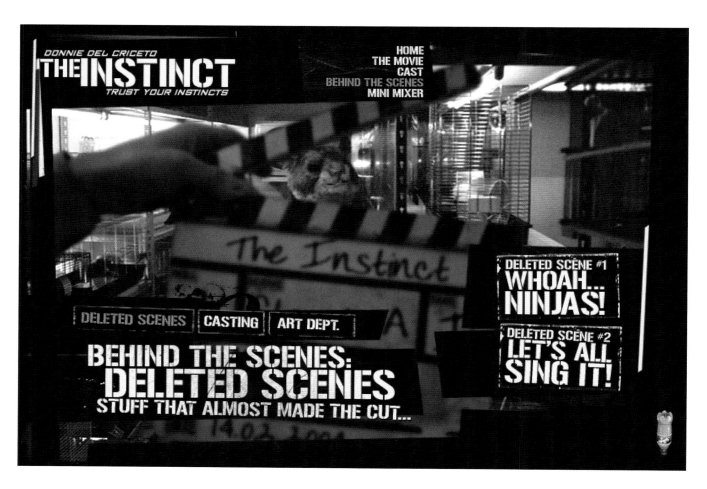

Agency
Framfab Denmark/
Copenhagen
Client
Coca-Cola Nordic
Art Director
Damian Claassens
Writer
Lewis Raven
Programmer
Philip Louderback
Content Strategist
Mikala Remvig
Designer
Jesper Bolther
Information Architect
Søren Schultz Hansen
Creative Director
Lars Bastholm
URL
www.theinstinct.com
Annual ID
05016N

The site's interactivity is very engaging. How did you approach the design of the site? We knew our target audience was movie- and movie Web site-savvy, but this was a double-edged sword. If we got the design and content right, we could familiarize our target audience with the concept more easily. Correct interaction and exploration would be second nature for them. If we got it wrong, it would be seen as a phony from the first sight of the homepage. So, we tried to utilize as much unique (non-TVC) imagery from the shoot as possible, blowing it up full-screen (a la all big budget movie sites) and emblazoning overly serious taglines across the shots at every opportunity. The idea was to create a rich, visual environment that would extend the story, making it seem like this was an experience based on a 100-minute epic and not a short TVC. The absurd film-noir theme that runs throughout the site, as well as the font and cut-away transitions were all meant to further this intrigue so users felt as if they wouldn't know the whole story, even if they had seen the TVC, until they had experienced theinstinct.com.

The site is an interesting blend of a movie promotion, DVD interface
and recording studio. Could you describe the origins of the concept?
Most of us won't encounter a massive, talking, bipedal hamster or dog in our lifetime.
As such, we thought it would be a shame to play down the concept potential by going down
a typical digital route, working purely within the specific physical and narrative confines
of the TVC. We didn't want to assume this was a fictional story that only existed for 30
seconds in a world on the box. We asked ourselves, "what if this wasn't an ad but a movie
based on real characters?" Well, that movie would need a name, a movie Web site, an
egomaniac of a director, a leading man/hamster, a bunch of failed actor/singers on the
periphery... Once we'd opened up our horizons, the content opportunities became endless.
The only problem then was deciding what we should leave out.

Where does the hamster motif fit into all of this?
The hamster motif is fundamental to the concept because it shapes and defines the
absurdity of the story. Whether you see the TVC or go to the Web site first, the huge, furry
sk8erboi is the most unique visual ingredient and it's this motif that will subsequently
embody anything and everything you remember of the experience. It's why we used the
silhouette interpretation so much; the idea being that Donnie should be omnipresent in
the experience, always there casting a shadow and repeating his message: whoever or
whatever you are, trust your instincts and be yourself.

POWER TO THE PEOPLE

Butler, Shine, Stern & Partners asked aspiring auteurs and creatives
to help them tell the Converse story. The only requirement was to send
in a 24-second short film—not commercial—heralding originality, creativity
and self-expression. In short, the hallmarks of the brand. The response
and range of creativity speak for themselves.

Agency
Butler, Shine, Stern & Partners/
Sausalito
Client
Converse
Art Director
Nei Sobral Caetano da Silva
Writer
Charlie Gschwend
Digital Artist/Multimedia
Zaaz
Designer
Nei Sobral Caetano da Silva
Creative Director
John Butler
URL
www.conversegallery.com
Annual ID
05017N
Also Awarded
Merit Award:
Corporate Image B2C . Web Sites

How did the Converse Gallery site originate?
We wanted everything that we created or had created by others for the campaign
to live somewhere, where it could easily be accessed by our consumers (we actually
call them members). The web seemed the best place for that.

How did you get the word out for submissions?
Was "word of mouth" a large factor?
We did a number of DVD solicitations that we distributed to film schools, and did
posters that we hung in and around film schools and universities. A few print
ads strategically placed in relevant magazines. Some communication to members
through the converse site. But mostly, each film that aired on MTV was tagged
with a submission solicitation at the end of the spot.

How many submissions did you receive?
Since August of 2004 the agency has received over 1000 submissions.

FILM INFO

STEPS

DREW HANCOCK

NATIVE MUSIC, WWW.NATIVEMUSIC.NET

> HOME

> SEND IN YOUR OWN FILM

> SIGN UP TO HEAR THE LATEST

> MOST WATCHED FILM

> WATCH THE NEWEST FILMS

> SEND TO FRIEND

> DIRECTOR'S COMMENTARY

> DIRECTOR'S BIO

> FEATURED SHOE

FILM GALLERY

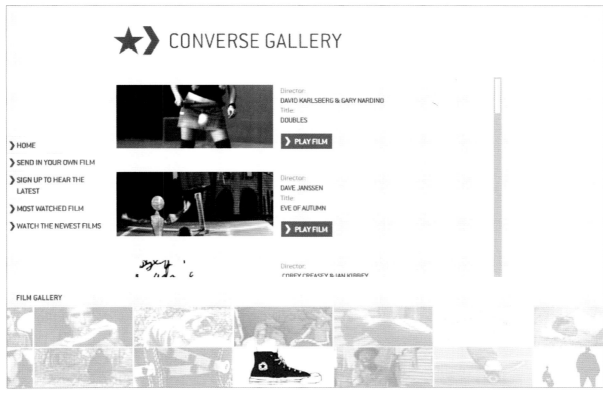

CONVERSE GALLERY

> HOME

> SEND IN YOUR OWN FILM

> SIGN UP TO HEAR THE LATEST

> MOST WATCHED FILM

> WATCH THE NEWEST FILMS

Director:
DAVID KARLSBERG & GARY NARDINO
Title:
DOUBLES

> PLAY FILM

Director:
DAVE JANSSEN
Title:
EVE OF AUTUMN

> PLAY FILM

Director:
COREY CREASEY & IAN KIBBEY

FILM GALLERY

SILENT FILMS
IN THE DIGITAL AGE

2001 Videolocadora, a DVD and VHS retailer, asked Loducca22 to promote the launch of Charlie Chaplin's complete works on DVD. What better way than to recreate a silent film? The completely original execution involves downloading a Microsoft Word file and vigorously hitting the "page down" key, putting into motion the considerable drama.

Agency
Loducca22/São Paulo
Client
2001 Videolocadora
Art Director
Erica Valente
Writer
André Piva
Programmer
Marcio Quartilho
Designer
Erica Valente
Creative Directors
Amaury Bali Terçarolli,
André Piva,
Celso Loducca
URL
www.lo-v.com/
oneshow/silent
Annual ID
05019N

What was the brief from the client and where did you come up with the creative idea?
Our client, 2001 Video, DVD and VHS rental and sale, asked us for a campaign informing their clients about the launch of Charlie Chaplin's complete works on DVD. The idea came out from the counter-point between Web technology and the simplicity of silent cinema. Then we tried to enhance the idea using the least technology sophistication possible. We developed a piece on a simple software that most users command with no major difficulty and that could be sent via e-mail therefore virilized through as many web users as possible. The final result was the script for a silent film illustrated with Microsoft Word characters, providing the user lucid contact with the essence of Chaplin's work.

Attachments carry the risk of getting rejected or ignored. Was that a concern?
The risk of being ignored was not a major issue with this project, since we used our client's database obtained from the official Web site registration. The user has registered and authorized 2001 Video to inform them of news via e-mail. So they were expecting e-mails from 2001 Video.

How was the response from the users?
10,000 users were impacted and 52% e-mails were virilized, leading our client to achieve sales goal.

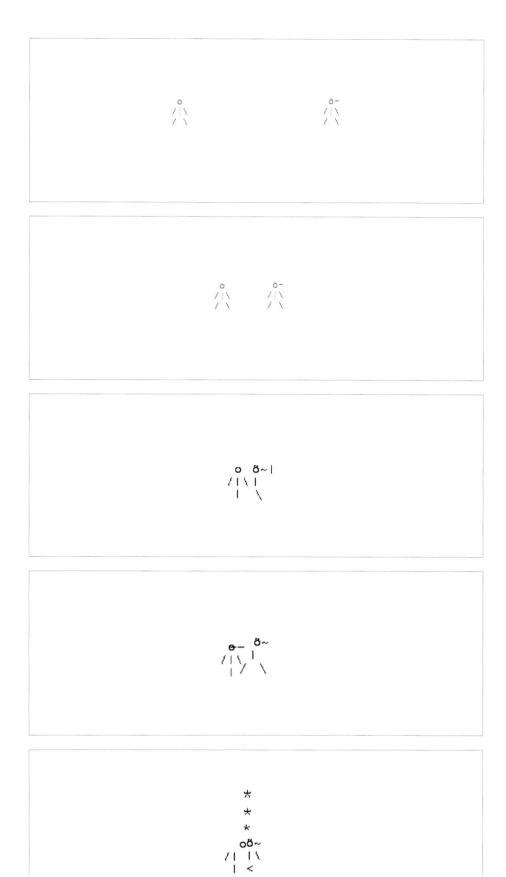

SASHAY

Utilizing near-perfect motion and superb navigation, Neue Digitale provides a superlative online consumer experience by way of a virtual catwalk for Yohji Yamamoto and adidas. The interface allows each model and outfit to be seen from three unique perspectives.

Agency
Neue Digitale/Frankfurt
Client
adidas-Salomon AG
Art Director
Bejadin Selimi
Writer
Lenore Appelhans
Digital Artists/Multimedia
Marc Freund, Michael Barnutz
Programmer
Jens Steffen
Designer
Bejadin Selimi
Creative Director
Olaf Czeschner
URL
www.neue-digitale.de/
awards/y-3
Annual ID
05021N

This work combines two brand names, Yohji Yamamoto and adidas.
Was that a challenge to reflect each brand identity and create a new joint brand?
The Japanese designer Yohji Yamamoto is known for his distinguished, simple, clear and elegant fashion style, and for his fabulous fashion shows, whilst adidas stands for sport and movement. These are the basic principles behind the Web site: the first Prêt-à-Porter fashion show on the Internet. Movement is shown through animation while the elegant look of the site reflects Yamamoto's style.

The concept of the Web site www.adidas.com/y-3 goes perfectly with the Y-3 brand: Models present the new Y-3 collection as they strut down a virtual catwalk. In the broadband version of the site, a randomly chosen model appears and presents an outfit. The user can view the models/outfits from three different angles.

What was the challenge in executing visual excellence and other technical aspects?
Achieving the desired simplicity was a challenge. A site that needs to display large
numbers of clothing items for men and women as well as shoes and accessories needs
to be integrated into a user-friendly interface which doesn't appear overloaded.

The designers solved the problem with a navigation that was complex in its conception,
but intuitive to use. In each case, only the relevant navigation is displayed, which ensures
a simple and clear view for the user and doesn't distract them from the fashion being
displayed. Only if the user actively requests more detailed content are further navigation
menu levels slickly loaded and displayed. This means that the user can reach any sub-
navigation menu point in just one click, without being hindered by long loading times or
too many menu levels.

How difficult was it to achieve the seamless motion of the models?
The video loop with the walking models was planned with the utmost care. The
designers built a dummy using the 3-D figure tool Poser, which provides the correct
walking movements for the three perspectives. Then the models had to strut down a
catwalk on a treadmill in front of a camera so that a clean, continuous loop could be
created in post-production. Any jumps were remedied using After Effects.

The loading time before the animation appears is bridged over by an animated silhouette
which consists of a vector curve. Then the animation of the front view of the model appears.
What appears to the user as a video is actually an animation of individual bitmap images.

As soon as the mouse-pointer moves over a model a grey arrow appears which rotates
around the model 3-dimensionally. The user can navigate to a different view of the model.
Further frame sequences are then loaded. The vector-animation covers up the time
taken to load the new sequences.

As a result, the user experiences a virtual fashion show on the Internet and can see
how the clothing from Y-3 really falls on the body.

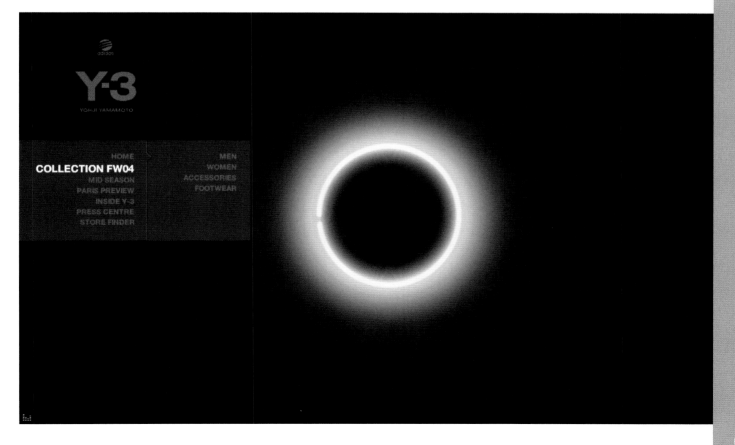

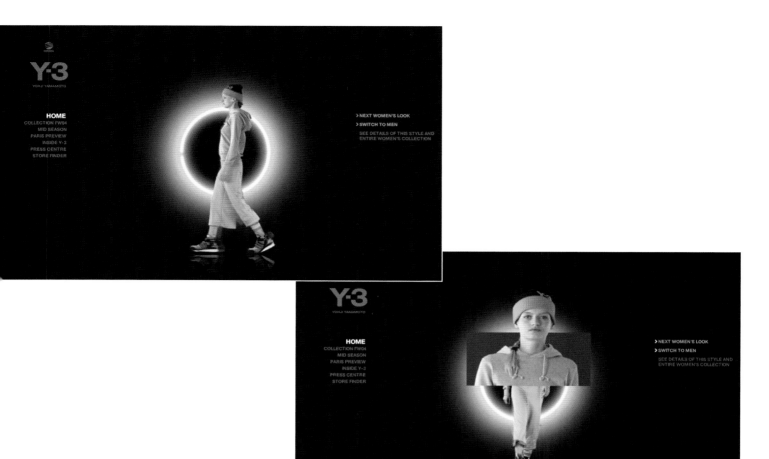

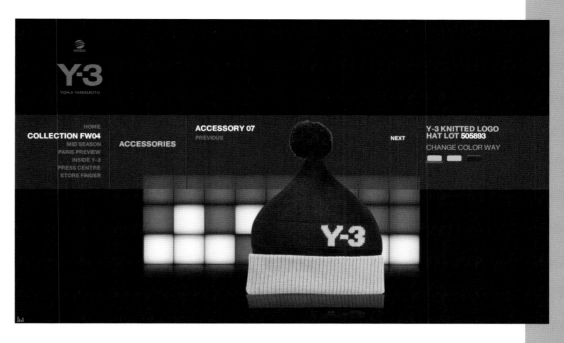

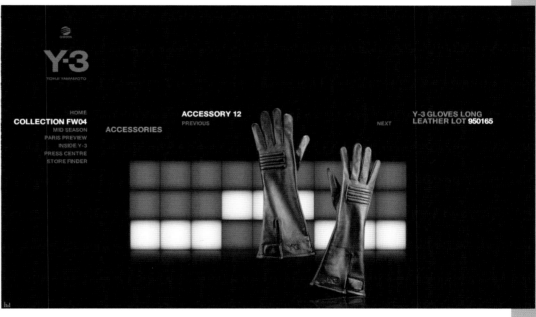

BIG IN JAPAN

Sponsored by Toshiba, Tokyo FM Broadcasting organized a large number of concerts by Japanese artists. They turned to Dentsu to promote the concert festival. Utilizing a map of Japan to visualize the schedule and content, Dentsu also created mini-sites for each of the performing artists with each artist's link placed at the city of their respective concert. The site is a content-rich yet graceful interactive experience.

Agency
Dentsu/Tokyo
Client
Toshiba Corporation
and Tokyo FM Broadcasting
Art Directors
Yugo Nakamura, Aco Suzuki
Writer
Aco Suzuki
Digital Artist/Multimedia
Yugo Nakamura
Programmers
Keita Kitamura, Akane Tsuchiya
Content Strategists
Yugo Nakamura, Koichiro Tanaka,
Aco Suzuki
Designers
Yugo Nakamura, Hisayuki Takagi,
Hiroshi Koike, Atsushi Fujimaki
Creative Directors
Aco Suzuki, Yugo Nakamura,
Ryohei Mitsuhashi, Masakatsu Kasai
URL
www.interactive-salaryman.com/
pieces/fmfestival/
Annual ID
05023N

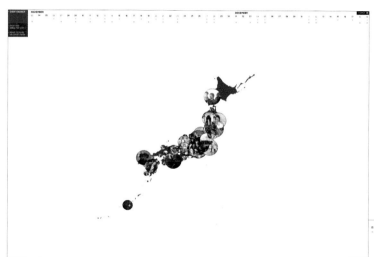

Can you describe the beginnings of designing the site?
To visualize the information on the events, which were held all over Japan and played by independent artists, we thought it'd be a good idea to use a map of Japan. We made this image as an interface where the time axis and the place information for each event could show up at the same time and interact with each other so that people would understand what was happening at that time.

What was the involvement of each media—interactive, radio, music—and how did they act together in the creation of this site?
Each media has its own culture. A challenge was to understand the differences in the production process in each media and to bring them all together on the Web. The radio station played a role as a community where fans could share information and their passion for their favorite artists. We made the most of what we have in each media by avoiding waste in order to create a whole new media.

What considerations did you face with the content of the artists' profiles within the mini site?
When you design a Web site, it is popular to make a whole Web site in the same tone. However, since we wanted artists to express their individualities, we asked them to prepare their original mini site without feeling any restrictions. Some visitors said that it's even cooler with all of the different tones.

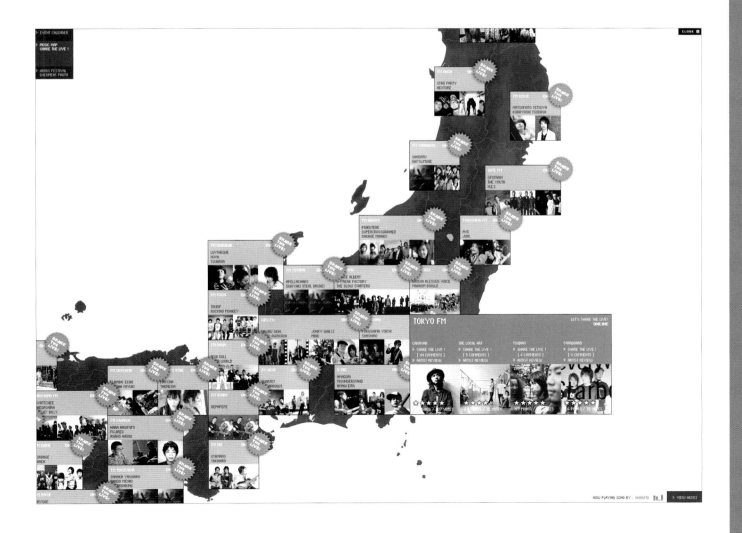

NO AGENCY
IS AN ISLAND

In an unusually collaborative effort, four agencies from three cities worked
together to create the topsy-turvy Aiwaworld. A saturated reflection of
the modern world, Aiwaworld explores the collision of disparate musical
genres and cultures and their influence on each other.

Agency
Wieden + Kennedy/London
Wieden + Kennedy/Tokyo
Hello Design/Los Angeles
Oceanmonsters/Los Angeles
THE_GROOP/Los Angeles
Client
Aiwa
Art Directors
+CRUZ, David Lai,
Jose Caballer, Jack Peng
Writers
Sean Thompson,
Joshua Homnick
Content Strategists
Sam Brookes,
Arto Hampartsoumian,
Ash Makkar, James Guy,
Kenshi Arai, Hisaki Kato,
Kenji Tanaka, Charlie Tinson,
Tony Wong, Frank Mele,
Sharon Tani, Szu Ann Chen

Can you talk about the rewards working with such
an array of creatives from different agencies?
It was truly exciting to collaborate with all the different agencies. We all really respected
each other's work and each brought our own strengths to the project, pushing each other
to do better work—a true synergy. Each agency also had specific roles so that it was clear
how things would work on an executional level.

Wieden + Kennedy London and Tokyo oversaw the overall branding campaign and concept,
Oceanmonsters created the various "hybrid music" videos, Hello Design developed a depth
engine to allow users to zoom in and out of different content bubbles, and THE_GROOP
was central at making sure all the pieces came together. Everyone was involved in the
creative development of Aiwaworld, from the "instrumals" to the Sonics. The hardest part
was probably working and communication with the different time zones. In the end, it was
well worth it.

How involved was Aiwa in the site's development? Did they have a brief,
give direction or were they really open to your vision?
Aiwa gave us a lot of creative leeway in the creative conceptualization for the entire
project. It is always a challenge to reach the youth market, and Aiwa relied on the creative
teams to come up with a great concept and execute it. The idea of an audio-visual world
filled with surprises tied in Aiwa products well without direct selling, which was key for
the client. It was about a bigger picture in creating that brand experience and engaging
our audience. It's not often where a client gives you the license to innovate and push the
boundaries, and we loved being able to do that for Aiwa.

There are so many layers to Aiwaworld.
How did the collaborative creative process work?
From the beginning the agencies worked together to brainstorm and develop the overall creative concept—create a zany, topsy-turvy audio-visual world, a youth network delivering "hybrid music" experiences lead by Wieden + Kennedy London and Tokyo. The Aiwaworld "container" was developed by THE_GROOP and Oceanmonsters, and Aiwa TV was Hello Design's focus. In the end, everyone had to work together to fine-tune and integrate all the elements, including the interactive pieces from artists Mumbleboy and Tokyoplastic, into the overall experience.

Programmers
Carlos Battilana, Eric Campdoras,
Aureliano Gimon, Pedro Leon,
Dan Phiffer, Arnaud Icard,
Roger Obando, Eduardo Polidor,
Will Amato, Scott Lowe, Martin Cho,
Damon O'Keefe
Digital Artists/Multimedia
Mumbleboy, Tokyoplastic
Designers
Hiro Niwa, Christel Leung,
Guy Featherstone, Yiing Fan,
Sun An, Paul Hwang,
Kellis Landrum, Rudy Manning,
Joshua Trees, Grace Chia,
Freda lau, Earl Burnley,
Saadi Howell, Ogo Kunio, Aldo Pucion,
Sophie Hayes, Nicholla Longley,
Michael Russoff, Lem Jay Ignacio,
Chaz Windus, Jorge Verdin
Creative Directors
Tony Davidson, Kim Papworth,
John C. Jay, Sumiko Sato
URL
www.hellodesign.com/aiwa
Annual ID
05022N

FORM
FOLLOWS FUNCTION

In the spirit of Vodafone's progressive product design, Hakuhodo i-studio creates a clean and decidedly futuristic site that features both existing and concept Vodafone models. The site is a testament to Vodafone's commitment to breakthrough design and the promise of imagination.

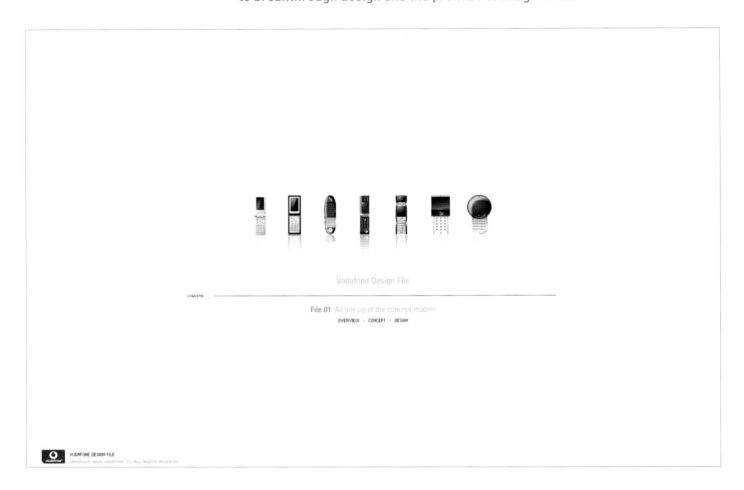

All of the Vodafones are beautifully designed. How important was it to have the site reflect Vodaphone the brand as a design leader?

Vodafone Design File is to introduce Vodafone's mobile phone design models. Many of them, however, are not in the market but merely concept models. So we needed not only to introduce the products but to visualize Vodafone's conscience toward designing. In doing so, the way to approach the user was extremely important, such as displaying the concept design in pictures and incorporating interactive functions.

The site has extraordinary usability in that you can disseminate content from so many perspectives. Can you talk about the actual organization of the site?

Rather than a visual inspiration, "file" is a metaphor of a tool to organize information with, as the site shows this concept in a boundless information cyberspace. Each page interactively introduces the model's style that stemmed from the key phrase "design from lifestyle."

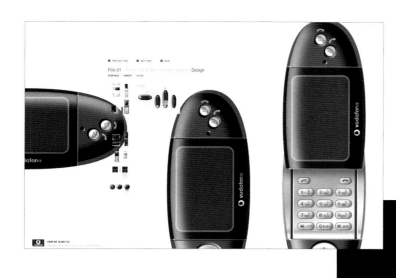

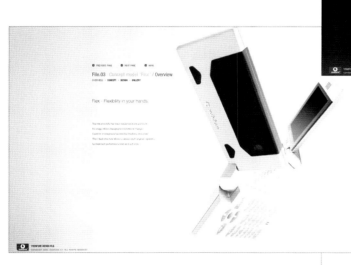

Agency
Hakuhodo i-studio/Tokyo
Client
Vodafone
Art Director
Katsuhiko Sano
Writers
Shunichi Oohigashi,
Atsushi Tanaka
Photographer
Ken Matsumura
Digital Artist/Multimedia
Takashi Morio, sin Inc.
Programmer
Takeshiro Umetsu
Designer
Katsuhiko Sano
Creative Director
Katsuhiko Sano
URL
http://award.i-studio.co.jp/
2004_vodafonedesign
Annual ID
05024N

AIR TRAFFIC CONTROL ON YOUR DESKTOP

By creating a real-time, downloadable screensaver that visually tracks all Germanwing's flights, Neue Digitale seeks to constantly connect people—be it at home or the office—to the airline. The sky changes in light and hue throughout the day and looks pretty nice on a desktop to boot.

Agency
Neue Digitale/Frankfurt
Client
Germanwings
Art Director
Bejadin Selimi
Digital Artist/Multimedia
Bejadin Selimi
Programmer
Heiko Schweickhardt
Designers
Melanie Lenz,
André Bourguignon
Creative Director
Olaf Czeschner
URL
www.neue-digitale.de/
awards/germanwings
Annual ID
05025N

How did the Germanwings screensaver concept originate?
The goal of the task was to keep the user in touch with the Germanwings brand—even when not online—and to increase ticket sales. Neue Digitale developed a screensaver and a tool to edit the content: a screensaver that shows a map of Europe with Germanwings aircraft flying over it, according to the flight plan. It also provides the user with up-to-date information and special offers, and promotes the Germanwings brand to those with itchy feet.

Can you talk about the challenges of programming the real-time flight information?
The most challenging requirement was creating a fully dynamic and customizable environment that reacts to multiple events that might occur at the same time or at least within a short period of time. Events such as announcing a departure or arrival, showing time-dependent campaigns, updating flight information and so on. Each one must be prioritized, queued and executed according to varying criteria, and handled individually. Because of the huge amount of data being processed and continually updated via the Internet, it was also one of the main challenges to create efficient calculation routines.

It seems like the aesthetic of the screensaver was very important
in that it is the desktop of someone's computer.
We chose a sky with white floating clouds as a background, since this is reminiscent of holidays and travel. The screensaver changes throughout the day and becomes darker at night.

The visual aspects of any screensaver are extremely important. The user practically allows the brand into their living room via the screensaver. But of course visuals alone are often not enough to enthuse the user. The functionality is important as well.

THE TIMES
ARE A CHANGIN'

Hewlett-Packard, a champion of innovation, sought to get people to think about change in a positive light rather than the knee-jerk foreboding norm. With colorful, jutting arrows and beautiful shots of metropolises, Goodby, Silverstein & Partners suggests that the only thing constant in the world of business is change and that our best choice is to embrace it.

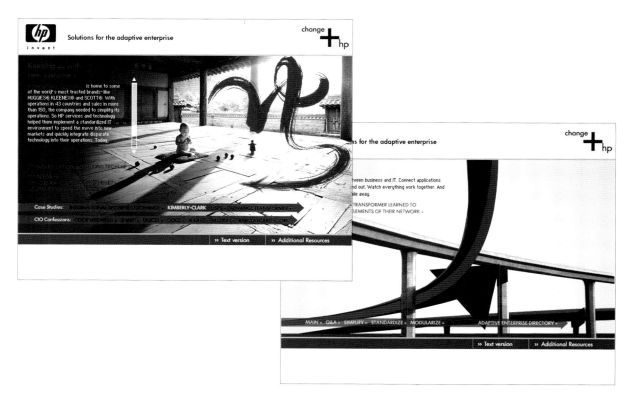

Agency
Goodby, Silverstein & Partners/
San Francisco
Client
Hewlett-Packard
Art Director
Merv Rey
Writers
Peter Albores,
Aaron Griffiths,
Tyler Hampton
Agency Producer
Brit Charlebois
Production Company
Number 9
Creative Directors
Steve Simpson,
Keith Anderson
URL
www.goodbysilverstein.com/
awards/adaptive_enterprise/
Annual ID
05026N

The Enterprise site represents just one service of the many that Hewlett-Packard provides to its clients. Was there a specific target audience?
IT managers and CIO level executives for medium/large corporations.

Given that most people resist change, was the concept to "Love Change" a difficult selling point even though it is conceptually appropriate?
In today's competitive business environment change is necessary for growth. Most people realize that, and are less afraid of change than what might have been found in the past.

The graphic language surrounding the change campaign evoked the sense of a movement that was starting. It presented the idea of change as a positive, energetic, revolutionary groundswell. Not a foreboding, scary thought, but an exciting one, that you could fall in love with.

The ubiquitous arrows of the site seem a natural way to signify the ever-changing world of business. What is less expected is how the arrows "build" the scenes of each page. How difficult was the actual programming of the site?
The programming of the enterprise site was challenging from the perspective that we wanted to provide a rich user experience, but knew that since our target audience is extremely busy, they would only have limited time to explore. Using the arrows to build the scenes of each page allowed for the customer to get a sense of energy of the campaign, while still providing them with the information they needed to find quickly.

Solutions for the adaptive enterprise

change
+hp

Simplify.

Reduce the number of IT elements in your network. Eliminate customization.
Automate change. Simplify everything and you are prepared for anything.

SEE HOW THE SCREEN ACTORS GUILD SIMPLIFIED THEIR IT INFRASTRUCTURE »

MAIN » Q&A » STANDARDIZE » MODULARIZE » INTEGRATE » ADAPTIVE ENTERPRISE DIRECTORY »

» Text version   » Additional Resources

Solutions for the adaptive enterprise

change
+hp

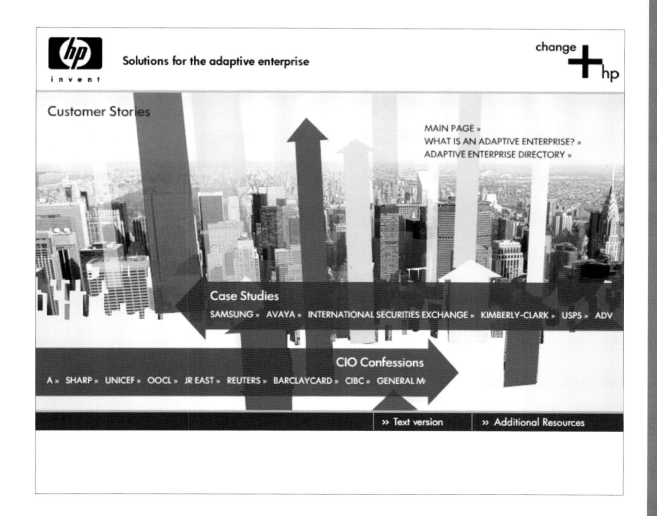

Customer Stories

MAIN PAGE »
WHAT IS AN ADAPTIVE ENTERPRISE? »
ADAPTIVE ENTERPRISE DIRECTORY »

Case Studies
SAMSUNG » AVAYA » INTERNATIONAL SECURITIES EXCHANGE » KIMBERLY-CLARK » USPS » ADV

CIO Confessions

A » SHARP » UNICEF » OOCL » JR EAST » REUTERS » BARCLAYCARD » CIBC » GENERAL M

» Text version   » Additional Resources

SILVER

CREATING A
CYBERSPACE
FOR SPACES

With sophisticated art direction and mindful design, TAXI strikes a balance of slickness and pragmatism for Diamond + Schmitt Architects, an environmentally sustainable firm with more than a few blue-chip clients.

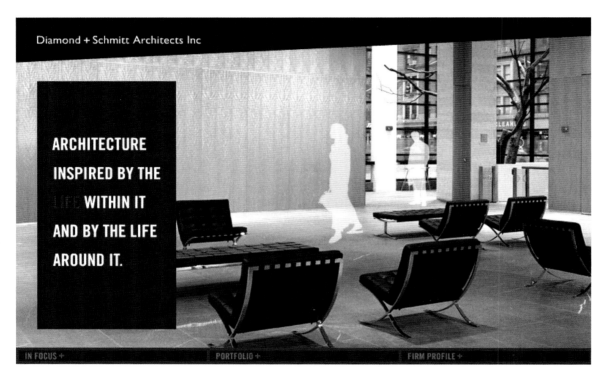

Agency
TAXI/Toronto
Client
Diamond +
Schmitt Architects
Art Director
Paulette Bluhm
Writer
Matt Rogers
Programmer
Matt Burtch
Creative Director
Steve Mykolyn
URL
www.dsai.ca
Annual ID
05027N

What was the brief from Diamond + Schmitt?

Diamond + Schmitt is one of the most accomplished architectural firms in Canada. We collaborated with them to raise the profile of their firm internationally and position them as serious competitors on the international, "super star" playing field. Diamond + Schmitt wanted to make a statement, show their thinking and showcase examples of their work as support.

How did the team come up with the creative idea and how did you execute it to represent the client company's style?

We created a positioning statement for Diamond + Schmitt—"Architecture shaped by the life within and by the life around it"—based on their long history of social activism in their work. Each of the case studies featured on the Web site provide a holistic perspective on the challenges faced by the firm and their approach to a number of unique problems. The voice of the founder and senior partner, Jack Diamond, was used to make a human connection with the work. Imagery was treated in a variety of ways to bring life to the portfolio. Finally, the plus-sign mnemonic used in their identity became a navigational element.

HP photo paper can resist fading

one third the width of a human hair

Agency
Modem Media/London
Client
Hewlett-Packard
Art Director
Albert Seleznyov
Writers
Julia Howe,
Paul Knott, Polly Jones,
Jeremy Garner

Designer
Dan Thorpe
Digital Artist/Multimedia
Ikem Okagbue
Creative Director
David Bryant
URL
modemmedia-awards.com/
hp-screensaver/
Annual ID 05028N

THE ART AND SCIENCE OF INK

Drawing attention to the science of Hewlett-Packard's Laserjet and Inkjet cartridge technology, Modern Media creates a visually striking screensaver of fluid ink coupled with copy that underscores two of HP's core values: technology and the environment.

Can you talk about your approach in terms of Hewlett-Packard's objective?
Hewlett-Packard wanted to raise awareness amongst its staff about the science behind HP LaserJet and Inkjet cartridge technology, together with paper and the company's environmental considerations.

Why was a screensaver decided upon as a solution?
The screensaver format allowed the information to be presented over a long period of time in "bite-sized" chunks. This meant that information which wouldn't normally be read was gradually embedded in viewers' long-term memories over time.

Each screensaver is graphically arresting.
Can you describe how the art direction was accomplished?
To attract viewers' attention, we had to make the screensaver as visually arresting as possible. The art direction uses short film sequences that are both relevant, visually rich and simple. The animation acts as a subtle hook to attract the attention of the viewer, whereupon they are presented with the facts in short, concise lines of copy.

MORE THAN
MEETS THE EYE

Building on the very popular "Build Your Own" MINI page on the MINI site, Crispin Porter + Bogusky decided to take the concept to the next logical step: customize your MINI Robot. After putting the finishing touches on your creation, e-mail it to your associates.

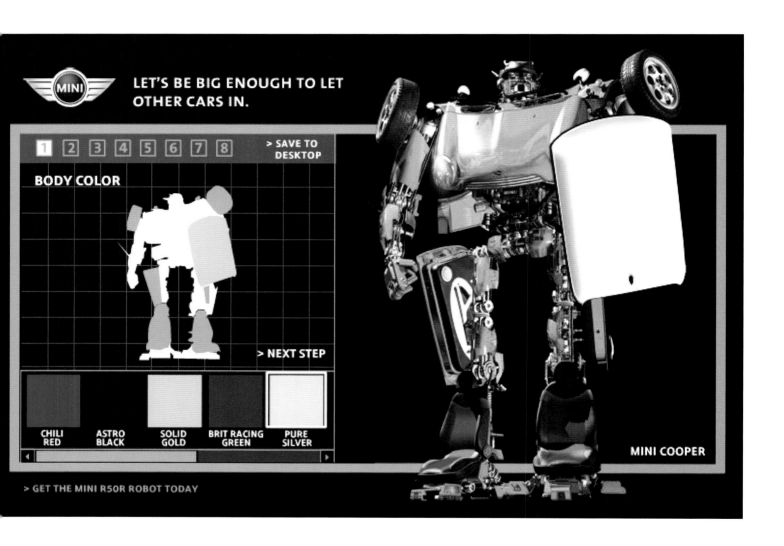

LET'S BE BIG ENOUGH TO LET OTHER CARS IN.

1 2 3 4 5 6 7 8   > SAVE TO DESKTOP

BODY COLOR

> NEXT STEP

| CHILI RED | ASTRO BLACK | SOLID GOLD | BRIT RACING GREEN | PURE SILVER |

> GET THE MINI R50R ROBOT TODAY

MINI COOPER

It's fun to customize a transformed Cooper on the Robot Configurator site. The site seems to be a cross between the "robot" billboards and the "customized" print work. Everyone felt very strongly about how well the R50R concept represented the true "spirit of motoring" almost like a sort of brand super ego that stood for many of the highest aspirations of the MINI mindset—being considerate of others, stepping up and doing the little things that, for better or worse, in this day and age, are often considered heroic. And then, of course, there's this extreme level of personalization that MINIs offer....and the robots in turn become this larger than life expression of that, with even all the inside pieces (seats, doors, etc.) out there for everyone to see.

On top of that, the "Build Your Own" section of the site has obviously been one of the most popular sections since it first launched in 2002, so the natural extension was to let people build their own MINI Robot.

How many hits did the site receive since its inception?
Unique visitors have been about 400,000 since it launched last year. Hits were very high (multi-millions) because each time you request a new part, that registers a hit.

A nice feature of the site is that you can save your finished robot as a jpeg on your desktop. Was there a sense of how many creations were circulated via e-mail?
No. It's hard to gauge exactly how many people might have sent their designs around but we do know that average visitor tended to design at least two, if not more.

Agency
BEAM/Boston
Crispin Porter + Bogusky/Miami
Client
MINI
Art Directors
Jamie Bakum, Dave Swartz
Writer
Bob Cianfrone
Digital Artists/Multimedia
Carlos Lunetta,
Sam Roach, ZOIC Studios
Programmer
Sam Roach
Creative Directors
Birch Norton, Andrew Keller,
Jeff Benjamin
URL
www.miniusa.com/open=
robotconfiguratorcooper
Annual ID
05029N

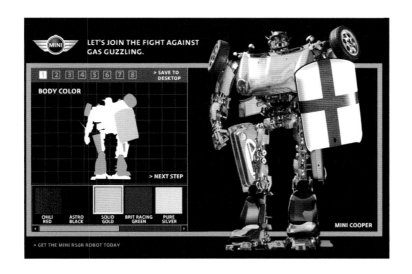

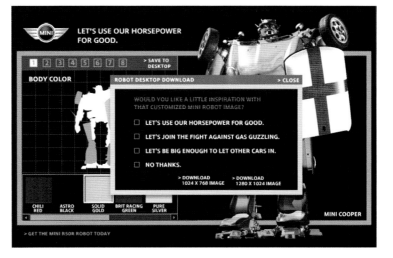

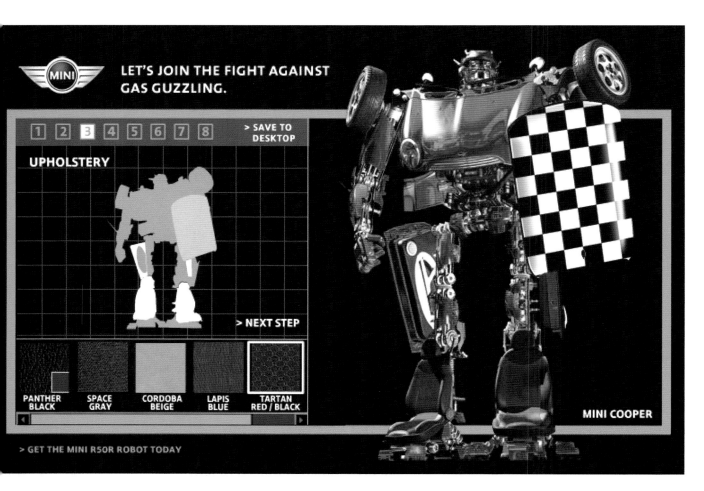

LET'S JOIN THE FIGHT AGAINST GAS GUZZLING.

1 2 **3** 4 5 6 7 8   > SAVE TO DESKTOP

UPHOLSTERY

> NEXT STEP

| PANTHER BLACK | SPACE GRAY | CORDOBA BEIGE | LAPIS BLUE | TARTAN RED / BLACK |

MINI COOPER

> GET THE MINI R50R ROBOT TODAY

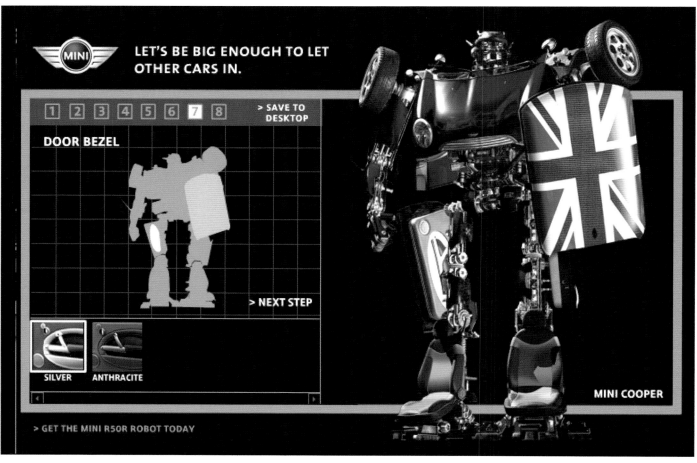

LET'S BE BIG ENOUGH TO LET OTHER CARS IN.

1 2 3 4 5 6 **7** 8   > SAVE TO DESKTOP

DOOR BEZEL

> NEXT STEP

SILVER   ANTHRACITE

MINI COOPER

> GET THE MINI R50R ROBOT TODAY

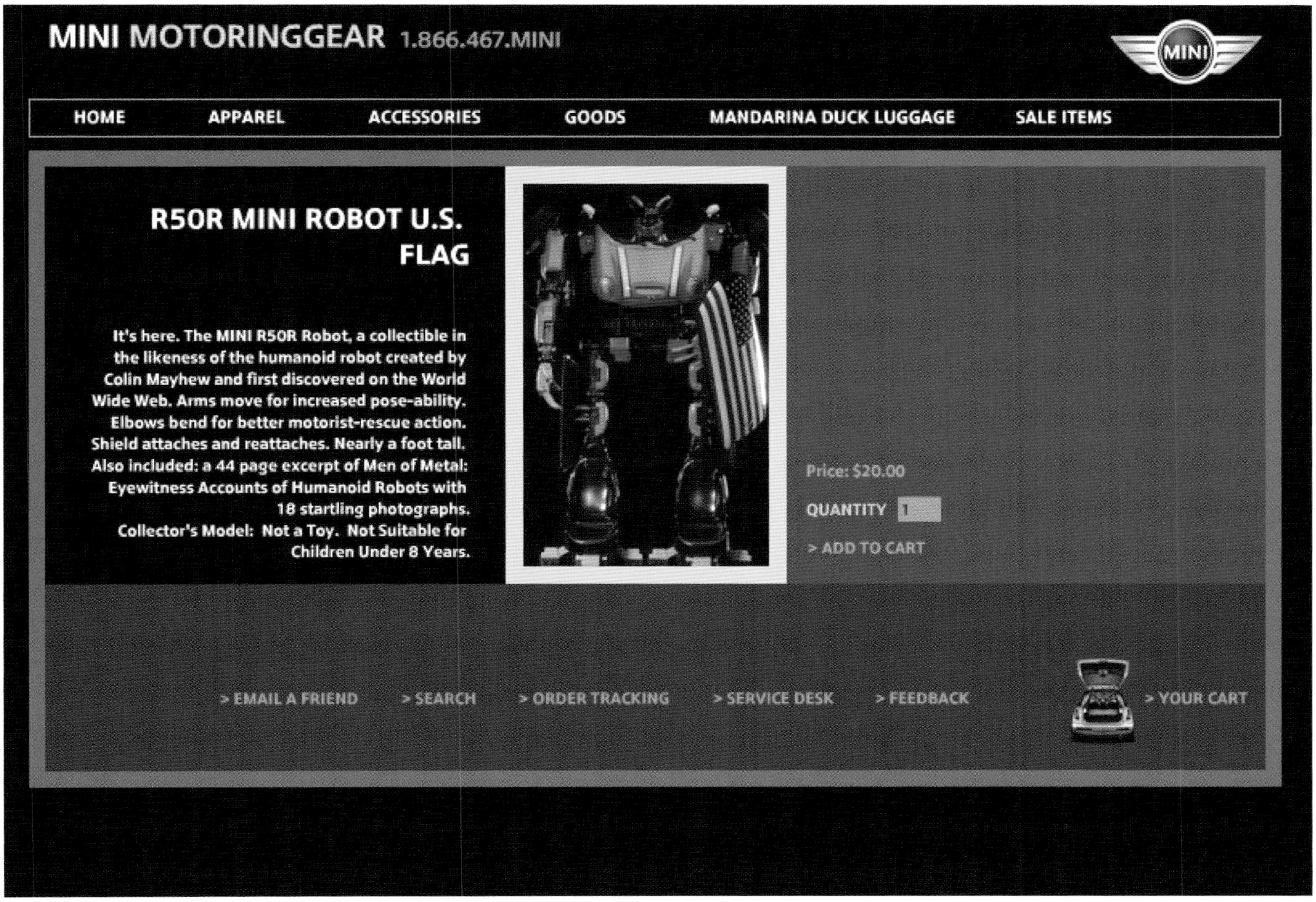

MINI MOTORINGGEAR 1.866.467.MINI

HOME | APPAREL | ACCESSORIES | GOODS | MANDARINA DUCK LUGGAGE | SALE ITEMS

R50R MINI ROBOT U.S. FLAG

It's here. The MINI R50R Robot, a collectible in the likeness of the humanoid robot created by Colin Mayhew and first discovered on the World Wide Web. Arms move for increased pose-ability. Elbows bend for better motorist-rescue action. Shield attaches and reattaches. Nearly a foot tall. Also included: a 44 page excerpt of Men of Metal: Eyewitness Accounts of Humanoid Robots with 18 startling photographs. Collector's Model: Not a Toy. Not Suitable for Children Under 8 Years.

Price: $20.00

QUANTITY 1

> ADD TO CART

> EMAIL A FRIEND   > SEARCH   > ORDER TRACKING   > SERVICE DESK   > FEEDBACK   > YOUR CART

DR. ANGUS,
LIFE STRATEGIST

In a timely parody, Crispin Porter + Bogusky introduces Dr. Angus and his Angus Diet. The Angus Diet is quite simple: eat as many Burger King Angus Steak Burgers as you like. The site features the very funny Angus Interventions page as well as the official, downloadable Angus Diet book. In the words of the man himself, "Waaayyyytagoooo!!!"

The Dr. Angus campaign is such a compelling spoof because it almost seems real. What was the thought process in virtualizing Dr. Angus?

There was a constant filter applied to the work. What would these guys really say? The stuff these "life gurus" spout out is so ridiculous anyway, it was pretty easy to find the balance between what would be funny and what would make it seem authentic. Alex pushed us to keep it very genuine. Harry Enfield was so damned funny in his Dr. Angus character. He just got it so fast. If anything we had to continually pull him back from going over-the-cheese-top. Sometimes we wondered if we were shooting ourselves in the foot, making it too boring. But in the end Alex was right. Again. The more real the better. With the book, however, it was about turning it up a notch. Finding examples to illustrate Dr. Angus' good-life philosophy that were just so stupid and ridiculous—like wrestling a supermodel, which I've done, and recommend.

Dr. Angus is not a real doctor.

Agency
Crispin Porter + Bogusky/Miami
Client
Burger King
Art Directors
John Parker, Kevin Koller,
Rahul Panchal
Writers
Evan Fry, Ryan Kutscher
Photographers
John Parker, Stock
Illustrators
Dwight Allott, Lin Wilson
Digital Artist/Mulitmedia
Loyalkaspar
Agency Producers
Rupert Samuel, Eva Dimick,
David Niblick, Sandy DeMouy
Production Companies
The Barbarian Group, Oddcast, ASD
Director
Harry Enfield
Creative Directors
Alex Bogusky, Andrew Keller,
Jeff Benjamin, Rob Reilly
Annual ID
05030N
Also Awarded
Silver Award:
Beyond the Banner . Campaign
Merit Award:
Corporate Image B2C . Web Sites

The psychobabble language employed by so many actual
"life strategists" is done to great effect. Once the concept was established,
the writers must have had a lot of fun with the content.

The writers had a hoot of a good time finding and writing in the Dr. Angus voice. A real
gas, you might say. Developing his characteristics was a great first exercise. What
would he speak like, what would he wear, what kind of things would he champion
and recommend with his "lifestyle-plan"? We were on the first video conference-call
with Harry Enfield and when we heard his fake American accent we totally loved it.
That helped it gel for sure. Once those character details came together, the voice
came together. Then we just rolled. Ryan Kutscher jumped in and wrote the Angus
Interventions on the site, for example, and he got it instantly. Of course he's this
brilliant statue of a man with a giant male organ, but still. Everyone involved had a
blast with it. Except for all the caustic stress and peptic ulcers.

Because it is a parody and also because it deals with people's health,
were there legal issues that arose?

How best to answer this? "F__k yes" should cover it. There were bucketloads of legal
issues. Lawyers slept under our desks. We had a stenographer outside office. The
crux of the very concept was the issue. That word: Diet. And with a big international
client like Burger King, they had no choice but to watch out. But we were always
impressed with their courage. It was such a bold idea to run with. We worked around
it with tons of disclaimers, which we didn't mind because they added to the humor
and reality of the work, but there were lots of lines from the TV that we had to pull at
the last minute. There were so many book rewrites it became a running joke. Adding
to this was the general climate of the time. There were people trying to sue fast food
companies for "making them" obese. Then there was a lobby group representing the
fast food industry that saw our cuts and kind of flipped out—imploring Burger King
to take out even more than we'd chopped before. Honestly, however, none of it hurt
the work. We were happy with how it all pulled together. Happy like clams. Cute little
clams on the bottom of the sea.

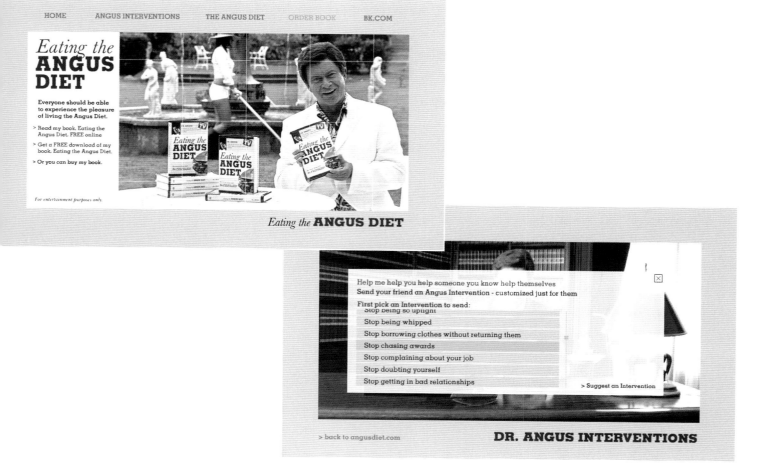

How to Eat Food That Tastes Good

Call me Mr. Crazy Pants if you wanna, but it seems to me that eating good-tasting food has become a lost art. I don't really know why, but I definitely notice a lot more people out there eating unfulfilling stuff than I used to. If you'd like to regain that lost art, The Angus Diet is for you. Here's how to do it. First, find some food that tastes good. The Angus Steak Burger fits this bill perfectly. And you can acquire one at any BK.* So do that. Next, open your mouth. Luckily this is automatic for most of us. Opening wide enough to fit The Angus, however, may require some warming up and stretching. Do this by repeating "OHIO" over and over again in exaggerated fashion. Ohio. Ohio. Ohio. Then go for it. Open wide and shove it on in there. Then simply use the muscles in your jaw to bite down on The Angus (the average human jaw is capable of exerting 1,200 pounds* of pressure on an object, so The Angus should be no problem). Separate a satisfying bite from the rest of The Angus and begin chewing (mouth closed, no smacking, thanks). Now you're eating food that tastes good. Practicing a lost art. That's living!

*I didn't check this stat as I find stat checking boring. So it could very well be way, way off.

Mouth Strengthening Exercises

1. Smile BIG. Try to get the corners of your mouth to touch your ears. You won't be able to, but try. Hold for five seconds.

2. Pucker your lips as though you're trying to suck mashed potatoes through a straw. Hold tightly for five seconds.

3. Hold your lips together and move them from one side of your face to the other. You should feel the stretch in your cheeks. And that's good.

4. Fill your cheeks with air. Hold for five seconds. Release. Repeat. You are a ball.

K.O. FOR BK

Pitting Burger King's two signature chicken sandwiches head-to-head in an interactive fighting game for world domination not only made a big impact among consumers, it was one of the key factors in declaring Burger King "Client of the Year."

Agency
Crispin Porter + Bogusky/Miami
Client
Burger King
Art Directors
James Dawson-Hollis,
Michael Ferrare
Writer
Rob Strasberg
Photographer
Kyla Kuhner
Illustrators
James Dawson-Hollis
Mike Koelsch
Digital Artist/Mulitmedia
Brand New School
Agency Producers
Rupert Samuel, David Rolfe,
Corey Bartha, Paul Sutton,
Eva Dimick, Jessica Hoffman

The concept of Chicken Fight seems very natural in that Burger King had two signature chicken sandwiches to promote. Can you recount the beginnings of the concept?
It started like every other fun concept, "wouldn't it be cool if we..." We were working outside at Haagan-Dazs tossing around ideas when we came upon chicken fights. Originally it was hot girls on our shoulders having a chicken fight in a pool. It somehow changed to two chickens fighting in a cage.

This idea really came together when we decided to make it The Chicken Sandwich World Championship free on Pay-Per-View. At that point we stopped looking at like commercials and went about promoting it like an actual heavy weight fight. Every piece of creative went thru that filter which gave the concept a definitive direction, the Web site, the promos (commercials) the fight poster (ads) and the event itself all had to stay true to this theme. Thankfully, Burger King is a great client who is willing to take risks and embraces new media or this idea would have just been some fun TV spots.

Most importantly, which is better, The TenderCrisp or the Spicy TenderCrisp?
Next year we're creating a sandwich to address this question. It's a 1/2 regular TenderCrisp and 1/2 Spicy TenderCrisp under one bun. We're calling it "Rumble in a wrapper." That way everyone can decide on the spot.

Production Companies
@radical.media,
Beacon Street (music),
Andrew Feltenstein,
John Nau, WDDG
Directors
Jonathan Kneebone,
Gary Freedman,
The Glue Society
Creative Directors
Alex Bogusky, Andrew Keller,
Jeff Benjamin, Rob Reilly,
URL
www.cpbgroup.com/awards/
chickenfight_int.html
Annual ID
05032N
Also Awarded
Silver Award:
Brand Gaming . Web Sites
Merit Award:
Corporate Image B2C . Web Sites

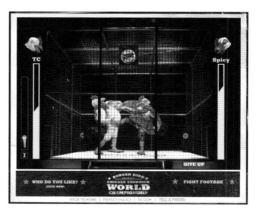

CAPTURING
THE INNOVATION
THAT IS HP

Through clever effects and high interactivity, Goodby, Silverstein & Partners expresses the inventive nature of Hewlett-Packard and bolsters the idea that "you +hp = anything is possible."

Hewlett-Packard is a behemoth in that it provides so many different services to such a cross-section of people. Can you talk about the challenge of creating a useful yet manageable site?

Since this was the first large-scale Flash experience to reside on hp.com, there were many self-imposed standards and objectives that had to be determined along the way. The first was establishing a file size limit that would allow us to have some fun, but that was also restrictive enough that it required us to be ingenious with how we used those precious kilobytes. We also had to keep in mind that we had to roll out the experience into fourteen countries worldwide—where we would often be dealing with slower download speeds and less bandwidth.

The goal behind each piece was to have the viewers feel the excitement of an inventive spark. The interesting thing is that we felt it ourselves through the fabrication of each piece.

The +hp campaign has been wildly successful. How did you approach the building of the site in relation to the previous creative work?

All of the +hp work is created from one core concept, and much of the work flows back and forth across mediums. We knew that we would need to provide more in-depth information about Hewlett-Packard partnerships than we could do in a print or TV ad, and the logical place to do that was online. We used the medium much broader and deeper than we did in previous campaigns.

What were the key objectives in the aesthetic both in terms of corporate identity and also navigation and usability?

From a corporate ID standpoint, the key objective was to brand Hewlett-Packard as a contemporary, energetic and revolutionary (and inventive) company. That philosophy meant that the traditional ideas of navigation (and usability) needed to be rethought and represented in a more engaging and interactive manner that also visually highlighted the breadth of the partners.

Agency
Goodby, Silverstein & Partners/
San Francisco
Client
Hewlett-Packard
Art Directors
John Norman, Todd Grant, Sean Farrell,
Hunter Hindman, Antonio Navas, Steve Yee,
Merv Rey, Will McGinness, Jeff Benjamin
Writers
Steve Simpson, Rick Condos, Mike McKay,
Tyler Hampton, Dan Rollman, John Knecht,
Matt Ashworth, Peter Albores
Photographers
Jim Marshall, Jonathan Minster,
Mike Elliott, Amy Guip
Digital Artist/Mulitmedia
Michael Chamorro

Agency Producers
Josh Reynolds, Lisa Gatto, Melissa Nagy,
Joni Wittrup, Sharon Kuerschner,
Michael Stock, Margaret Brett-Kearns,
Mike Geiger, Amanda Kelso
Production Companies
Paranoid Projects: Tool, H.S.I.,
Natzke Design, The Barbarian Group
Directors
Francois Vogel, Paul Hunter
Creative Directors
Rich Silverstein, Steve Simpson,
Keith Anderson, John Norman,
Hunter Hindman, Rick Condos,
Antonio Navas, Will McGinness
Annual ID 05033N

SILVER

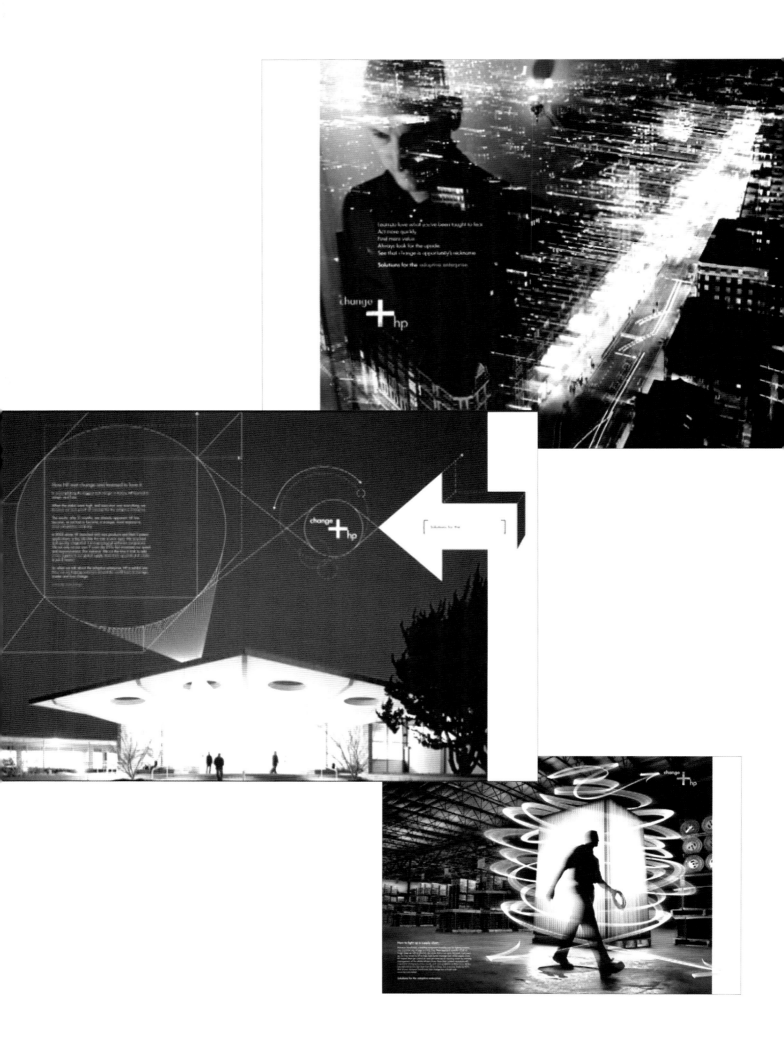

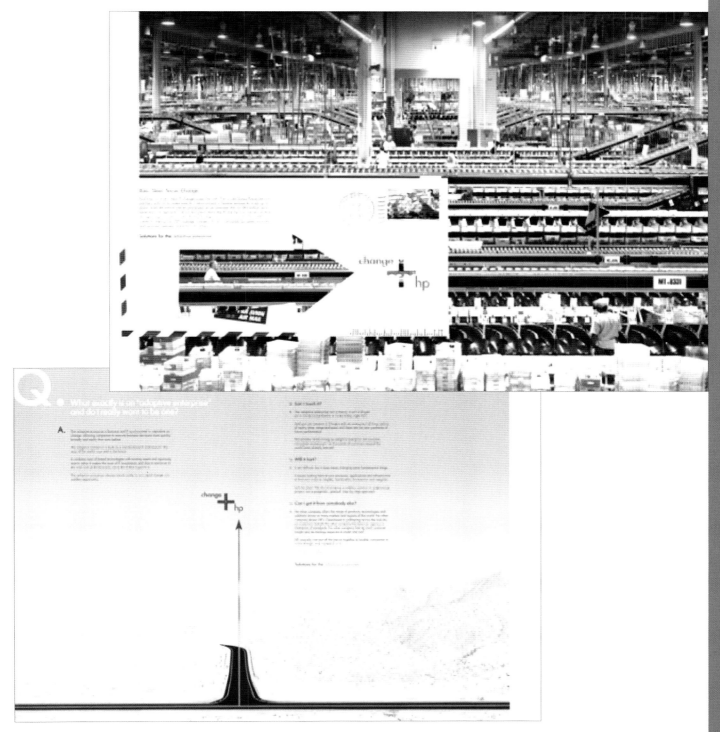

YOUTH GONE WILD

Part competition, part scavenger hunt, SS+K rounded up groups of students, armed them with an inflatable mascot and released them into the city with their Qwest phones as their only tool. Semacodes were sent to the students on their Qwest mobiles with clues on where to take their mascot and ultimately achieve victory.

Agency
SS+K/New York
Client
Qwest
Art Director
Josh Kilmer-Purcell
Writers
Maya Frey, Roman Tsukerman
Illustrator
Studio AKA
Digital Artists/Mulitmedia
Kevin Slavin,
Cary Gibaldi (Invisible Inc.)
Programmers
Dennis Crowley (ubiquity labs),
Simon Woodside (Semacode Inc.),
Kevin Cancienne
Agency Producers
Kevin Slavin, Elizabeth Cioffi
Content Strategists
Kevin Slavin, Frank Lantz
Designers
Gemma Mitchell,
Alice Ann Wilson,
Brian O'Neal
Information Architect
Kevin Slavin
Creative Director
Marty Cooke
Annual ID 05034N

What were the challenges in orchestrating a campaign of such diversity and scale?
If we'd known how many obstacles there were, we might never have dreamed up Conqwest. We had to learn everything about the municipal zoning laws in five cities, the dynamic effects of heat, cold, trees and strong wind on 15-foot inflatable animals, the infrastructure of the entire Sprint SMS/MMS backbone and the optical distortion in phone cams. Plus, the coverage, physics and strengths of urban PCS network towers, the discrepancies between satellite photos and GPS information, etc.

And then there was the issue of building the technology infrastructure from scratch since the phones hadn't caught up to the technology when we started. What was originally designed for client-side Symbian phones had to be restructured to server-side Java MMS decoding, with PHP scripts to route thousands of messages through the game engine...

Each event could have been brought down by the slightest unanticipated problem, whether it was the phones themselves, servers, the game software we built, PCS tower availability, the decoding software we licensed, the local infrastructure we were running on or the awakening MMS backbone. Each event had 10 people headquarters just to deal with every one of these contingencies, all of which came up at least once—and sometimes all at once! To give you some idea of the complexity, here's what the technology contingency plan, dubbed the Panic Plan, looked like. (see page 113)

Where did the idea of pitting high schools against each other in the spirit
of competition come from?
We knew from studying videogame behavior that kids were familiar with and preferred
group or "clan" competition. If we could get a lot of kids to play, the game would be
more fun and more visible, which was part of the goal. Also, we knew from earlier
precedents within the Big Game genre that mass urban games worked.

Once we'd settled on the idea that the game play would involve large inflatable
animals, we needed groups of people to move them around. Given all the other
logistical problems, we wanted to find some ready-made groups. Since the target was
high school kids, it just made sense to go right to the high schools. That gave us ready-
made organization and focus as well as pre-formed interschool rivalries to amp up the
competitive juices. This also ended up being an angle that the media grasped easily in
their coverage.

This campaign is unique in that it seems to be striving to simply create
brand awareness for Qwest. Can you describe Qwest's brief?
I'd actually say Qwest's goal was to create brand preference rather than brand
awareness. That, and p.r. Qwest's product offering was relatively modest in a market
defined, at least to teenagers, by the latest bells and whistles. Add to this, that to a
high school kid, Qwest—if she's aware of it at all—is her parents' phone company. Not
cool. Not hip. But high school students are in a phase of life in which they're trying to
get prepared for real life. This gave us our "in." By emphasizing a Qwest cell phone's
toughness and reliability, we could make it more relevant than a more faddish phone.
Running around with wild, albeit fake, animals and discovering clues in the real world
suddenly made Qwest relevant and cool to a whole new audience and also made data
services relevant in ways they had not been.

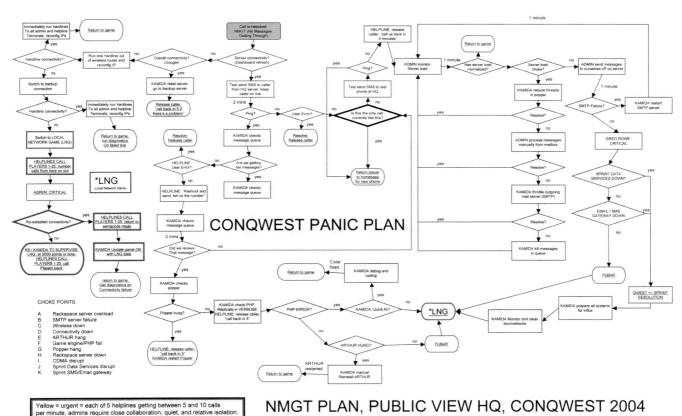

NMGT PLAN, PUBLIC VIEW HQ, CONQWEST 2004
FIRST DRAFT, 30 MARCH; Kevin Slavin, Michael Sharon

MINI DECLASSIFIES ROBOT R50R

With shades of Roswell and stunning effects, Crispin Porter + Bogusky creates intrigue and brand awareness for MINI and blurs the line further as to what is advertising and what is reality. If the effects alone aren't enough to give one pause, the site features Dr. Colin Mayhew and his invention, the MINI R50R Robot, which is mired in rumor.

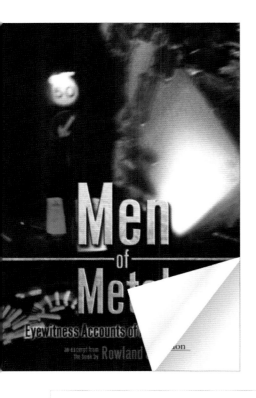

The object on the left was removed from a train track, 20 yards from the sighting on Botley Road. It has been identified as the tailpipe of a Mini Cooper (above) based on its classic beer can shape.

On my second visit to www.r50rd.co.uk/research/internal/v2i/engin/, I found several of Dr. Mayhew's drawings. They appear to be a blueprint for some sort of robot. One image (top right) is consistent with the depressions found after two of the sightings.

When I met with Mrs. Graham, I asked her to draw a picture of what she had seen. Her sighting, February 3, was the first on record.

I downloaded this image from www.r50rd.co.uk/research/internal/v2i/engin/ and showed it to both Horace Burrowes and Pelham Stevens. Each felt the object was similar to what they had seen.

25 - MEN OF METAL

Her story was similar to the others. Like Horace Burrowes and Pelham Stevens, she had her encounter when she was in danger. In her car. On the road. At night. She too saw a large object, maybe 15 feet tall, and as it left, it was going like the clappers. And she had no idea what she had seen.

I ask her if she managed to take a picture. She says that at the time, taking a picture was probably the last thing on her mind. I ask if she got a good enough look at it to draw a picture of it. She says she'll try. I give her paper and pencil, and after a few minutes, she presents me with a drawing.

I'm not exactly sure what I'm looking at. But whatever it is, it's looking back at me.

Before we get in our cars, I ask her one more question.

"Mrs. Graham, when the object left your car, in which direction was it traveling?"

"I don't know. Down Iffley Road, so I suppose westwards."

February 27.

"Here you go. It's an Oxford number."

I write it down.

"And the address?"

"2438 Binsey Lane."

"Thanks, Michael," I say. "Give my regards to Anna."

I have a mate at the phone company. I don't ask him for many favors, but when I do, he usually comes through. I ring Dr. Mayhew's number.

"Hello?"

The voice sounds like the voice of a 65-year-old man.

Agency
Crispin Porter + Bogusky/Miami
Client
MINI
Art Director
Dave Swartz, Paul Keister,
Juan-Carlos Morales
Writers
Bob Cianfrone,
Roger Hoard, Mike Lear
Illustrator
Daniel Hartz
Programmer
Jason Soros
Agency Producers
Rupert Samuel, Dan Ruth,
Sebastian Gray, Jessica Hoffman,
Loni Peristere, Steve Schofield,
Julieana Stechschulte
Production Companies
ZOIC Studios, Atomic Props, BEAM
Creative Directors
Alex Bogusky, Andrew Keller,
Jeff Benjamin
URL www.cpbgroup.com/
awards/r50r.html
Annual ID 05035N

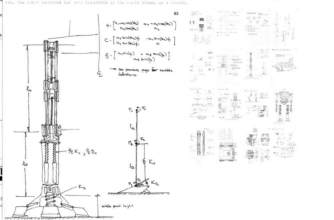

BRONZE

NEIGHBORHOOD KALEIDOSCOPE

With an urban, psychedelic backdrop, Syrup showcases Sony Style's product line with a parade of neighborhood characters. The Wishmaker section of the site allows users to select featured words from the dictionary to form a sentence serving as a holiday wish which later appears in a Sony Style storefont window.

sony style

Sony Holiday Window Design 2004

Agency
Syrup/New York
Client
SonyStyle
Art Directors
Erik Jarlsson, Kim Granlund
Writer
Robert Holzer
Illustrator
Christopher Ehrnooth
Digital Artist/Mulitmedia
Andreas Brännström
Programmers
Mike Manh, Mark Lontsman
Agency Producer
Jacob Cohen
Content Strategists
Robert Holzer, Jacob Cohen
Production Company
Omino Gardezi (SAM LLC.)
Designers
Kim Granlund, Erik Jarlsson
Creative Director
Jakob Daschek
URL
http://www.syrupnyc.com/
clients/sony/index.html
Annual ID
05036N

How did you arrive at a solution of creating characters and profiling their life in relation to the product?
We looked at Sony products as defining a new "digital lifestyle" that affect people in very real ways: Someone could take a picture of their newborn baby and send it to relatives on the other end of the world in an instant through advances in technology and Sony is leading the way in making this possible. We wanted this digital lifestyle to be visualized through the people using the products rather than just the products themselves. We then tied this idea to creating "alternate-universe" holiday/winter scenes that would be visually striking.

The Wishmaker page of the site underscores the "connection" motif of the site. Could you describe the creative process of that particular page?
The Wishmaker is the component that ties the project together. The user is actually interacting with the installation in the store windows and getting to control the installation's message and identity at a particular moment in time. This element is really what makes the Sony Style Holiday Wishes project come together. Being able to send unique, personal messages from any computer to any SonyStyle store across the country. We wanted people to feel that technology can connect them to others (an aspect of technology that is often overlooked). By creating the site in Flash we were able to build an environment that engages the audience in a new way. We saw it as a kind of high-tech magnet art, that people play in groups while at a party so we included, along with the normal holiday words, a selection of odd adjectives and nouns to give people move creative freedom.

FOR SOME, GAMING IS IN THE BLOOD

To communicate the idea of "Forever Wireless" and to attract users to the new mobile developers Web site "Code-Blood," AgenciaClick created a banner featuring a game tattooed on a burly man's forearm.

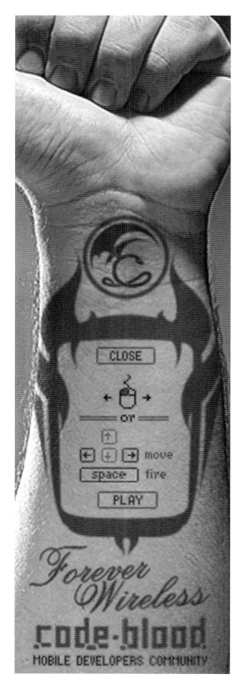
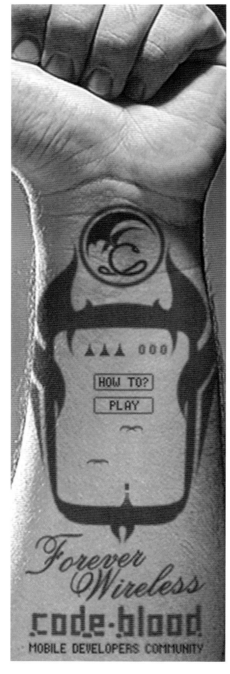
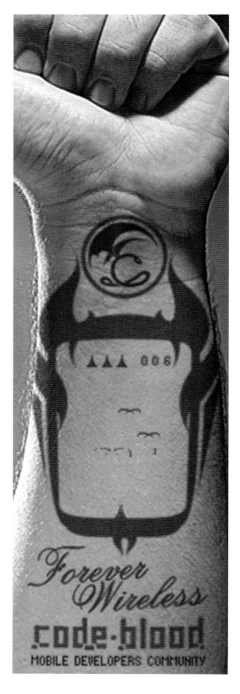

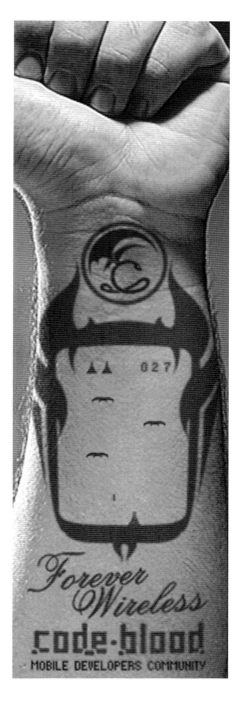 

Agency
AgenciaClick/São Paulo
Client
Instituto Nokia
Art Director
Flavia Campos
Writer
Andrea Costa
Photographer
Kazuo Okubo
Digital Artist/Mulitmedia
Arthur Guidi
Programmer
Fernando Aquino
Designer
Felipe Bastos
Creative Director
Ricardo Figueira
URL
www.virtualsofa.net/tattoo
Annual ID
05037N

Can you describe your approach for the site in terms of targeting the programming community?

The agency had a communication strategy to attract the users for the new mobile developers community Web site, but also create a remembered brand experience.

Why did creating a Space Invaders-type game seem like the best solution?

We choose to create a strong concept showing how mobile technology is integrated with the people. We believed that the tattoo image with the title "Forever Wireless" would translate it perfectly. It needs to be simple and at the same time viral and fun. So, we constructed a brand communication based on entertainment.

What was the response to the banner?

The ad game brought Nokia Institute a very big audience with high clicks levels and consolidated a strong identity with the new brand for the community called Code-Blood and powered by Nokia Institute.

THE CULT OF GURU

Influenced equally by the Italian Renaissance and Monty Python,
Diesel captures the devotion of Guru cyclists with a site that is
informative and entirely too much fun.

You can choose one of two roads: the Righteous Path, which has important
information about Guru and the Fools Route, which features two irreverent
and fun games. How did this dichotomy take form?

Pretty simple. Too many sites try to make a user experience that's both informative
and entertaining at precisely the same time. That can be pretty damn distracting.
We just thought it would be a good idea to separate the two up front, letting users
decide for themselves which road they want to take.

Can you describe the creative process involved with 'Face Wash' and 'Run for Your Wife?'

The Guru print campaign included a series of ads that had some pretty funny headlines. Two in particular had some serious creative potential for doing something really cool and entertaining in a web context:

"Biking can teach valuable lessons about focus and perseverance. Not to mention the importance of turning your head to spit."

"There's nothing like a long, quiet bike ride to get away from it all. Unless the wife also happens to enjoy long, quiet bike rides."

Using these as a springboard, we thought up a couple of simple games (Face Wash, Run For Your Wife) that would serve as a great backdrop for some ridiculous animations, some of which we made up as we went along.

From there, we decided that a Monty Pythonesque approach would be hilarious, so we took a few naked renaissance figures, dressed them in biking gear and let our imaginations run amuck. This crude, old-school animation style helped maintain the vintage tone that runs throughout the site.

In terms of content, we went for something a little risky in order to garner attention. That's why we decided to be quite graphic and, in some cases, disgusting, knowing that even if it turned some people off, it would at least get them talking.

The site is beautifully art directed with references to Italian Renaissance paintings and illuminated manuscripts. Can you talk about the aesthetic approach for the site?

The concept behind the Guru Bicycles campaign is that for the serious biker, riding is akin to a religious experience—one that encompasses devotion, passion and meditation. Hence the idea of putting bikers in rich renaissance environments, many of which were taken directly from original religious paintings and manuscripts of the time. Beyond the religious connotations, however, the paintings and manuscripts gave the site an air of timelessness and luxury, which is precisely what the Guru brand is all about. After all, these guys handcraft impeccable, made-to-measure frames that last you a lifetime. Unless, of course, you're a really, REALLY crappy biker.

Agency
Diesel/Montreal
Client
Guru Bicycle
Art Director
Cameron Wilson, David Lee
Writers
Jonathan Rosman,
Cameron Wilson
Illustrators
Cameron Wilson, Luc Normandin
Digital Artist/Mulitmedia
Cameron Wilson,
Christian Ayotte (animation)
Programmer
Christian Ayotte
Designers
David Lee, Cameron Wilson,
Jonathan Nicol
Creative Director
Daniel Andréani
URL
www.showmeto.com/gurubikes
Annual ID
05038N

GOLD

WHEN NINJAS ATTACK

In a multi-player, strategy-based action game, Big Spaceship invites players to pick a character and devise a series of moves to lay waste to the competition. The game is almost riveting enough to make you forget it's a promotion for 20th Century Fox's feature film, "Elektra."

The Elektra Ninja Assasin game seems like a cross between chess and a traditional action game. Can you talk about the concepting process and designing the mechanical aspects of the game?

There are certain limitations to building multi-player games with Flash. The differences in processor and Internet connection speed users can create problems with any real-time interaction in such games. Turn-based game models are more successful. In an attempt to reduce the time spent waiting for an opponent to move, we decided to let all users enter their moves at the same time. Not only does this keep the game moving along, it also has a significant influence on the strategy of the game, and it allows for the number of players to be increased beyond two, without affecting the wait time.

As opposed to some other promotional games, Ninja Assassin seems relevant to promote Elektra the movie in that they are both action based. Was it immediately apparent that a game was the best way to promote the movie?

It seemed like a great fit when we began concepting the game as both the film and the marketing materials were highlighting the individual skills and warrior mysticism of the characters within the film. Additionally, we felt that a straight, first-person fighting game would not do the film justice, as strategy also played a huge part in the fight sequences—knowing your opponents strengths and weakness and choosing a path that best complements your own fighting style, for example, was what we found relevant in both the film and the game.

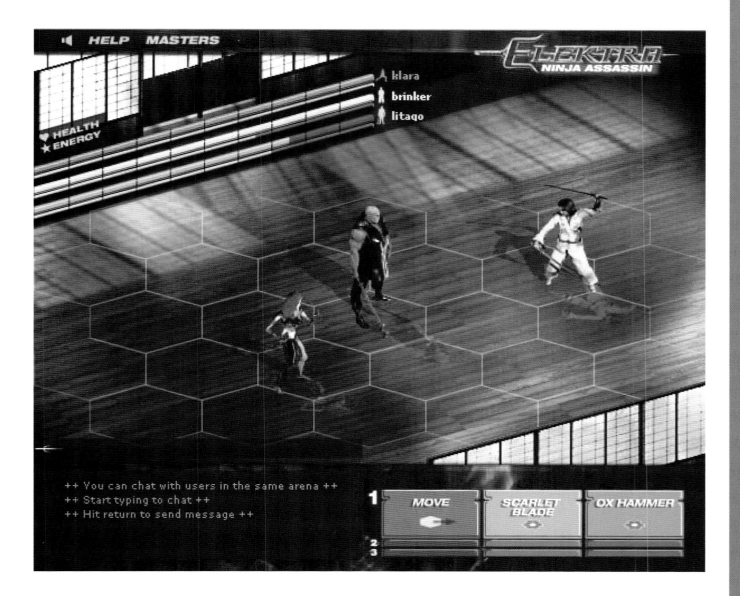

Agency
Big Spaceship/Brooklyn
Client
20th Century Fox
Art Director
David Chau
Writer
Karen Dahlstrom
Programmer
Joshua Hirsch
Creative Director
Michael Lebowitz
URL
game.elektramovie.com
Annual ID
05039N

The characters that inhabit the Elektra world have superhuman abilities so over-the-top action was necessary. Given that complete real-time Flash gaming is not yet possible, we decided to have users choose three moves in advance while trying to prognosticate their opponent's moves. Once the moves were locked in, the on-screen Elektra characters would attack, block, and energize their ways through battle. The multiple types of attack added variation and satisfaction to fans hungry to lay the smack down on another fellow gamer.

What type of feedback did you receive after it went live?
Shortly after launching the game, we had to add more game rooms multiple times to accommodate the number of users logged in. There were consistently anywhere from 200 - 400 users playing the game at any given time, logging hours and hours of game play. We found message boards with threads devoted to the game.

Seven months after the launch, this game is still drawing in multitudes of users back for more. Now other clients are clamoring, "We want a game like that." So, clearly the feedback has been positive.

SILVER

ART IMITATES LIFE

The Uniroyal Fun Cup is a 25-hour race featuring over 100 identical cars competing across 5 countries. To promote the actual competition, WM Team crafted a highly addictive racing game where you can compete with your friends to discover who will clinch the checkered flag.

Agency
WM Team/Hannover
Client
Uniroyal
Art Director
Rainer Michael
Writer
Rainer Michael
Designer
Rainer Michael
Creative Director
Rainer Michael
URL
80.237.207.52/funcup/
Annual ID
05041N

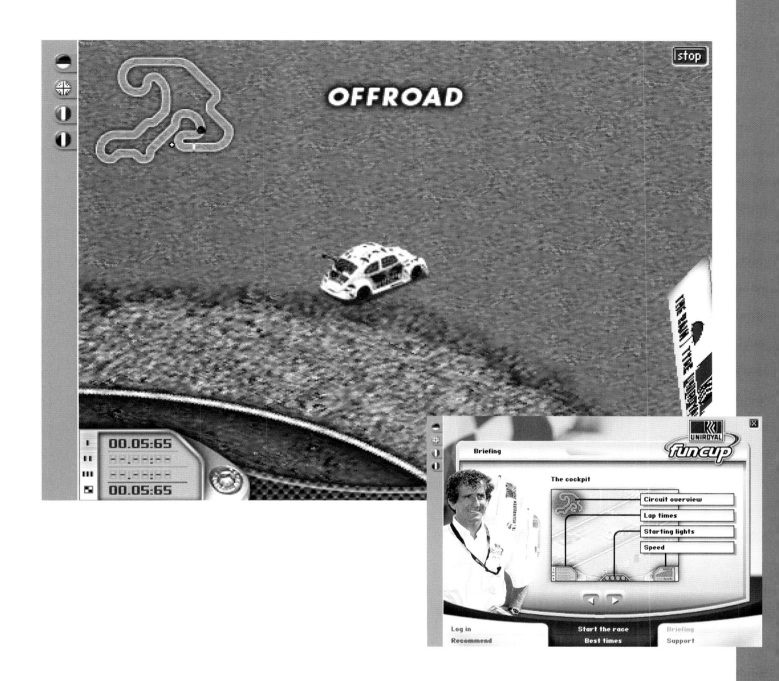

The site obviously promotes the Uniroyal Fun Cup through a fun, interactive racing game. Was the game concept approach an attempt to "spread" the game in a viral-like fashion from friend to friend?
We always try to do games or Web sites that spreads within the Web community because of its quality. In this case, there are a very few viral tools built in the game. It's a perfect game to invite friends and see who's the best racer.

Was it possible to measure the "spread" of the site?
The recommended feature was used about 8,700 times. We have over 31,000 registered users and many more guests. So, we can only guess how much users got a recommendation via standard e-mail or saw the game featured in a game-portal.

How did your core audience, the die-hard racing fans, react to the game?
We had a good reaction both from die-hard racing fans and general public. There were many users who came from the Uniroyal brand Web site and got into the game very quick. Anyway, we had several requests from users who wanted to buy the full version of the game for their PC.

Over all, there where over 4.2 million games played until today and I think that is a quite good reaction.

LEARNING TO FLY

Crispin Porter + Bogusky and BEAM teamed up to introduce
the MINI convertible with a long jump-type game where missing
the mark is oftentimes more entertaining than hitting it.

The game seems to fit very well with the rest of the work done for the MINI brand.
Was this site part of the initial campaign to introduce the convertible Cooper or did
its creation snowball from that campaign?
This game was part of the original launch campaign and was concepted back
in the summer of 2003, when we were thinking of all the ways we might introduce
a MINI Convertible. Then it was actually one of the first pieces to really kick-off
the official launch in the fall of 2004.

When you miss your landing there are some painful looking angles at work.
How were you able to recreate the human movements?
We used a fairly basic 3-D modeling program called Poseur but it got the job done
very effectively. We knew right way when we were conceiving this thing that, if we
built it right, we could have a game where failing might actually be as entertaining
(or even more so) than succeeding. This is a fairly rare thing in games, so we were
excited about its potential.

Agency
BEAM/Boston
Crispin Porter + Bogusky/Miami
Client
MINI
Art Director
Jamie Bakum
Writer
Birch Norton
Digital Artists/Mulitmedia
Mike Wislocki, Andrew King,
Marc Leuchner
Programmers
Mike Wislocki, Sam Roach
Creative Directors
Birch Norton, Jeff Benjamin
URL
http://miniusa.com/
?open=jumpgame
Annual ID
05042N

A SHOT IN THE DARK

Farfar thought the best way to promote a Nokia N-Gage and the latest game releases for Nokia's hand-held gaming device would be Blindfolded Boxing—a game where blindfolded pugilists try to punch each other's lights out. Create a boxer profile, record a sequence of punches, and let the action unfold.

Where did the idea for the Blindfolded Boxing game come from?
We wanted to show the luxury of being able to challenge anyone anywhere, a feeling well known to those who own a Nokia N-Gage. And what could be more challenging than trying to punch someone out with your eyes blindfolded? We can't really remember how the actual idea came about.

When you are locked in a room with your work mates trying to come up with a great idea, the impulse of hitting someone comes naturally after a few hours.

How many hits did the site receive?
Since launch the site has had about 17.6 million hits by over 250,000 unique visitors.

Agency
Farfar/Stockholm
Client
Nokia N-Gage
Art Director
Jennie Arvenäs,
Jakob Swedenborg,
Nicke Bergström
Writer
Henrik Berglöf
Digital Artist/Mulitmedia
Anders Gustavsson
Programmer
Bo Gustavsson
Content Strategists
Janne Lindforss,
Matias Palm Jensen
Designers
Erik Norin,
Rickard Lundberg,
Per Hansson
Creative Director
Jon Dranger
URL
http://www.farfar.se/
OneShow2005/
blindfoldedboxing_game
Annual ID
05043N

CAUGHT IN THE NOODLE

glue reminds viewers that Pot Noodles are sinfully good in a hide-and-seek game where a jealous girlfriend rushes into the living room hoping to discover a tawdry affair with noodles. The mission is to hide the noodles and pray she doesn't find them.

Agency
glue/London
Client
Pot Noodle
Art Director
Richard Glendenning
Writer
Simon Parkin
Programmer
Simon Cam
Designer
Simon Cam
Creative Director
Seb Royce
URL
www.gluelondon.com/
awards/2005/oneshow
Annual ID
05044N

How many different scenarios did you have to shoot?
The game works by your girlfriend searching more thoroughly on each progressive level, so that on level 1 she only looks in one place but by level 4 she looks in 4 out of the 5 possible hiding places. We ended up shooting about 20 scenarios (although we had quite a few takes on some of those). From those 20 we used 14.

The site was definitely a success. Were you able to track the average amount of time?
We did various bits of tracking both on the Noodle web (the whole site) and the game itself. The average amount of time on the game was just under 2 minutes. On the wider site it was closer to 8.

Agency
Pop & Co/New York
Client
Cartoon Network
Art Director
Jesse McGowan
Programmer
Howard Wakefield
Creative Director
Vincent Lacava
URL
www.cartoonnetwork.com/
games/powerplay/
calling_titans/oa.html
Annual ID
05045N

CLASH OF THE TITANS

With characteristic high production value, Pop & Co brings to life
the Cartoon Network phenomenon "Teen Titans" in an action-packed,
multi-player game. In the words of Puffy AmiYumi, "If your heart is
black, you better watch out/you cannot escape the team."

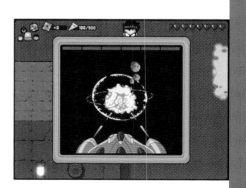

SHORT CUTS

Envisioned as a kind of "mini Cannes," a festival for mini mobile movies, Orange launched the Paper Film Festival for fledgling directors everywhere. Participants chose a genre to enter, downloaded a paperkit on the Orange Web site to create characters and scenes, and the rest was left to their imagination and Orange mobile.

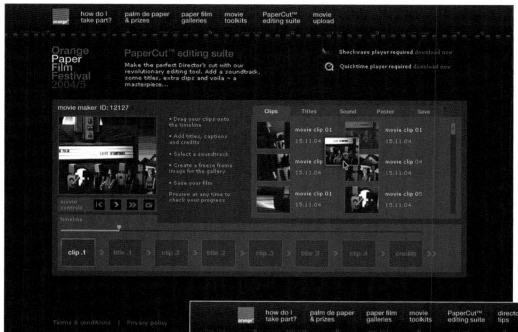

Agency
Poke/London
Client
Orange
Art Director
Steve Pearce
Writer
David McCandless
Digital Artists/Mulitmedia
Poke, playerthree
Programmer
FullSix
Content Strategists
Nick Farnhill, Niku Banaie
Designer
Steve Pearce
Information Architect
Nick Farnhill
Creative Director
Nick Farnhill
URL
www.paperfilms.co.uk
Annual ID
05046N
Also Awarded
Merit Award:
Beyond the Banner . Single

Orange
~~Paper~~
Film
Festival
2004

Palm de Paper
~ 2004/5 ~

How did the idea for the film competition come about?

This idea came about from a desire to prompt people to think creatively when they use photo-messaging—a desire to do something more creative with standard mobile technology—with a totally original application. So, why not have our very own Cannes festival for mini mobile movies? The 'Paper Film Festival' was born, with the 'Palm de Paper' as the prestigious prize. With six movie genres to choose from, users made the scenes and characters from paper kits downloaded from www.paperfilms.co.uk. A starter kit of primer tutorials, photos and movies were made by us to get people motivated and inspired. Users upload their scenes from their mobile, and then edit them online, adding music, titles and transitions in a specially designed Shockwave application. Once completed their entry was submitted into one of the three galleries: mobile films, video films and photo posters, awaiting the judging process. It all added a bit of fun, creativity and glamour to photo-messaging.

Orange has a reputation for great creative. What was it like working with them?

Orange share the same will to innovate and a desire to experiment with technology. Originality and ideas are paramount and people love seeing new approaches to existing products and services. Orange allowed us to push these ideas over boundaries that are seldom crossed.

Are there plans to make the competition an annual event?

There's always a possibility, but at the moment we'd rather come up with another new, exciting idea—to push ourselves and Orange further!

SALARYMAN ODDITY

The Japanese term "salaryman," means "a certain Japanese businessman who works hard, is always quiet, serious, and looks a little bit odd." Using "Salaryman" as a platform, Dentsu showcases a new collective of Creative Directors—Interactive Salaryman—delivering an "odd" but "sparkling" site.

Agency
Dentsu (Interactive Salaryman)/
Tokyo
Client
Interactive Salaryman
Art Directors
Yusuke Kitani, Hiroki Nakamura
Writer
Yasuharu Sasaki
Digital Artist/Mulitmedia
Hiroki Nakamura
Programmer
Hiroki Nakamura
Content Strategists
Yasuharu Sasaki, Aco Suzuki,
Hiroki Nakamura
Designer
Yusuke Kitani
Information Architect
Hiroki Nakamura
Creative Directors
Naoto Oiwa, Yasuharu Sasaki
URL
www.interactive-salaryman.
com/pieces/is_e/
Annual ID
05047N

How did you come up with the two culturally specific themes, "salaryman"
and "shateki"?
We hit on the idea of "shateki" (Japanese hitting game) immediately when we decided to
build Interactive Salaryman. We thought "shateki" would make the most sense in terms
of function and humor of the page since both "salaryman" and "shateki" are such
traditional Japanese aspects. And, don't you feel like poking, or hitting someone when
he/she did some enviable work?

What spurred the creation of the site?
Our writer's English teacher who always told him that Japanese people should express
more about themselves.

How much involvement did the directors featured on the site have with the site itself?
As you see, all directors appear in their self-promotion mini movie once selected.
But their action was directed by us and they were forced to act as they were told.
If they were involved with the planning, we would have no idea how many Web sites
we might have!

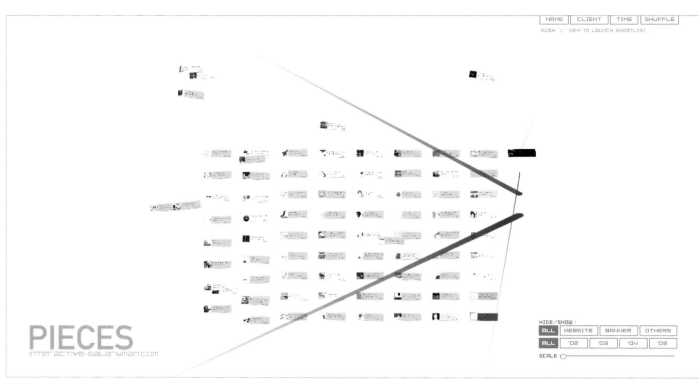

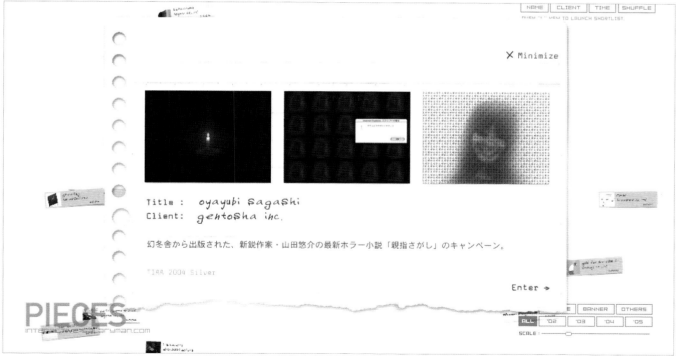

A CORNUCOPIA
OF DESIGN

Largely inspired by video game iconography, one-man agency HYBRIDWORKS's Web site is a veritable smorgasbord of design and illustration. Heavily influenced by food and the seasons, fans return to download screensavers and icons celebrating various earthly delights.

Agency
HYBRIDWORKS/Tokyo
Client
HYBRIDWORKS
Art Director
Masaki Hoshino
Digital Artist/Mulitmedia
Masaki Hoshino
Programmer
Masaki Hoshino
Designer
Masaki Hoshino
URL
www.hybridworks.jp/
Annual ID
05048N

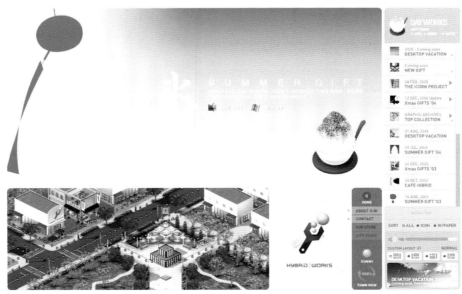

**Your site is an amazing showcase of your animation.
Where does your inspiration come from?**
I keep a close watch on video games around the world, including those developed
in Japan. In fact, I rarely play video games these days, but I'm greatly influenced by
their graphics, settings, movement, and the like. I have many favorites among the
works created by Pixar Animation Studios, because they blend realism with humor.

**The Simcity-esque community window is a great feature in that it changes
with each section of the site. Where did this idea originate?**
I was inspired by a detailed diorama of a railroad I saw when I was a child. The
diorama had a mechanical device with a button that could move miniature trains
and people, and the sun could be turned down to simulate night. I remember that
just looking at the diorama gave me a pleasant feeling.

HIGH DESIGN FOR TALL BUILDINGS

For Office Use Only faced a monumental assignment in organizing a site to accompany MoMA's Tall Buildings exhibition—a survey of 25 buildings, some actual, some purely conceptual, organized by height. The site itself, however, approaches the content from multiple perspectives: each building has an individual profile page; the Heights Comparison Page provides structural perspective; and the Design Issues Pages focus on aerodynamics, egress, emergency exit routes and green technology.

Describe the brief you were given by MoMA.

We were given the published exhibition catalog and a briefing on how the physical exhibition would be laid out. Whether we stayed closely with the content and structure of these existing components or proposed something new was up to us, as long as we could justify it.

Since For Office Use Only has built a working relationship with MoMA for over 4 years and has stocked their trophy case with numerous design awards, there's definitely a level of trust they have in working with us.

In doing research, we realized that the exhibition had a single organizing principle: present the 25 buildings in the show from the shortest to tallest. We felt that this was interesting, but ultimately we decided, aren't buildings 25 and 24 and 23 getting short shrift? And in this linear organization, it's a bit difficult to see why building 18 is connected with building 9. Why are those two buildings in the same show? So basically we came to the conclusion that the site shouldn't just present one comparison (height) but compare area or program or use of green technology or geographic distribution, etc. By focusing on a kind of comparative analysis, we could show these buildings as not just being tall, but address many social, technological, and urban issues that make this genre of building relevant.

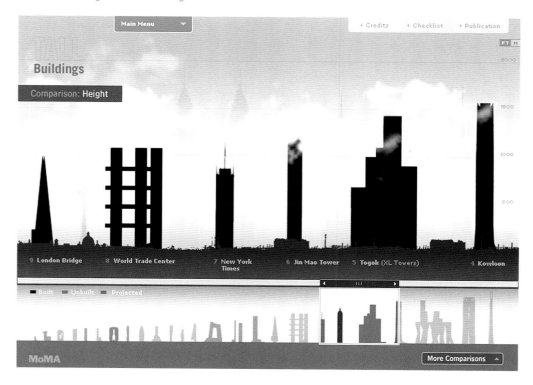

Agency
For Office Use Only/New York
Client
The Museum of Modern Art
Art Director
Anh Tuan Pham
Programmers
Anh Tuan Pham, Chris Lasch,
Kimba Granlund
Content Strategists
Anh Tuan Pham, Chris Lasch
Designers
Anh Tuan Pham, Chris Lasch
Creative Director
Anh Tuan Pham
URL
http://www.moma.org/
tallbuildings
Annual ID
05049N

What were some of the challenges that you faced?

In developing a Web site that differentiated and strayed from the main structure and threads of the exhibition catalog, we more or less had to "generate" and organize much of the content ourselves. That is, we had to create detailed spreadsheets of building data to determine what comparisons were compelling and do-able. We had to start making connections between buildings to one another and plan the means of providing context and commentary so that those relationships were clearly communicated. I'd say as much as 75% of the content and info of the site wasn't given to us from MoMA. It was all taken from us comparing data, making connections, and working with the MoMA curators to articulate the new written content.

How did the client/public respond to the site?

The curators and the Digital Media department were thrilled because we provided them with a look at the exhibition that they just didn't anticipate. I got an e-mail from the chief curator, Terence Riley, and he essentially stated that the Web site provided new sets of connections and contexts that he hadn't realized. We've heard from the MoMA staff that during the exhibition, the on-site kiosks were often filled with people, which isn't common when you can just see the exhibit first-hand. It seemed the site provided something beyond the experience of the physical exhibition itself.

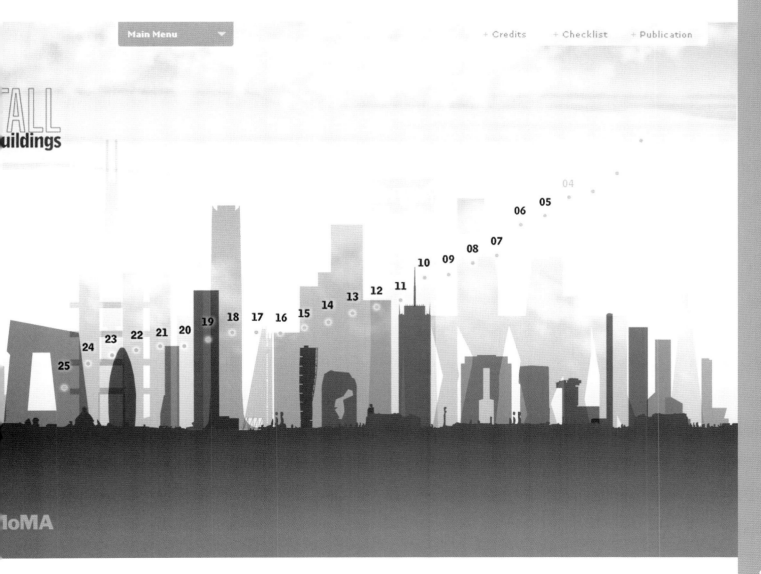

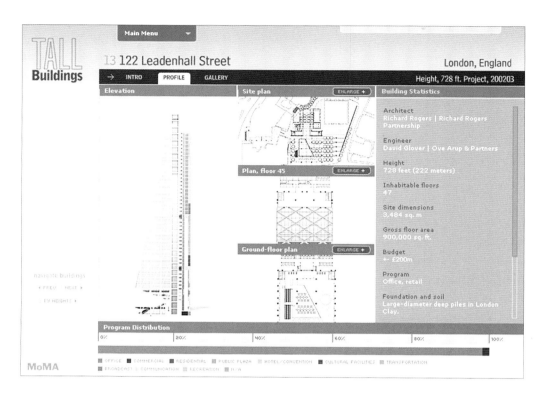

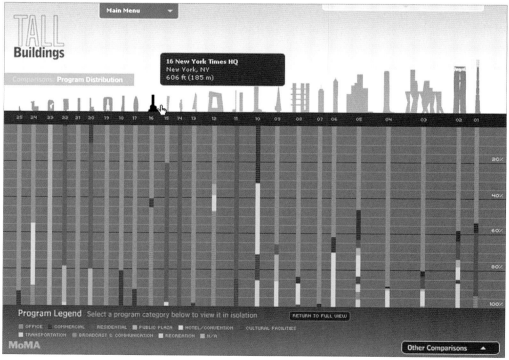

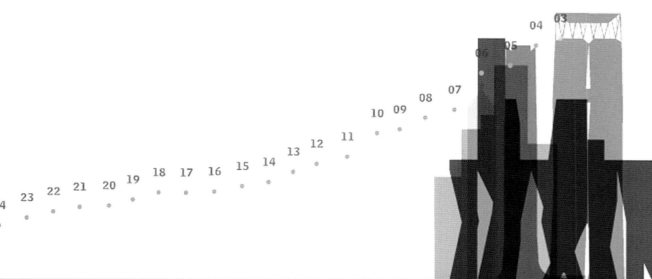

Loading Tall Buildings

MoMA

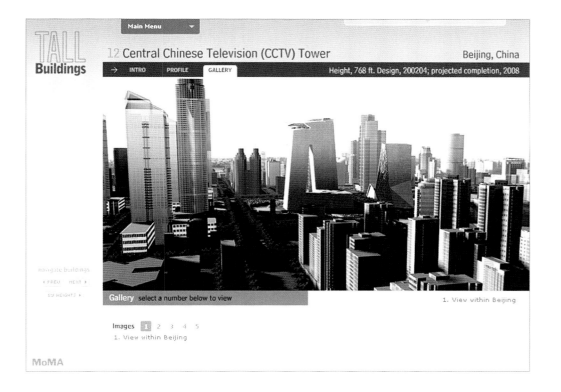

GOLD

THE UNKNOWN MINK

Fork Unstable Media honors the countless animals consumed in the fur industries with a sober and serene execution for NOAH. A floating strip of glowing vigils, the site invites the public to write an epitaph and to learn more about the fur industry. The site illuminates the power of the Web's medium, bringing activists together the world over.

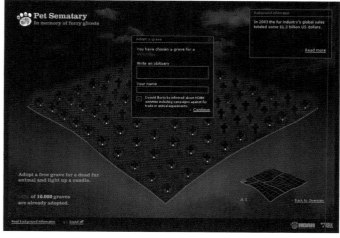

Agency
Fork Unstable Media/
Hamburg
Client
NOAH Menschen für Tiere e.V.
Art Director
Anna Mentzel
Writers
Holger Illing, Tons May
Digital Artist/Mulitmedia
Christophe Stoll
Programmer
Florian Finke
Content Strategist
Roman Hilmer
Designer
Tilo Göbel
Creative Director
Christophe Stoll
URL
www.petsematary.de
Annual ID
05050N

**The concept is very elegiac and noble and uses the media
in a very innovative way. What was the genesis of the concept?**
NOAH - Menschen fuer Tiere e.V. requested us to develop an idea calling public
attention to the revival of fur in fashion. Our idea stands on the assumption that there
is no need putting straight that animals in fur farms are being cheated out of their
lives and cruelly killed. A lot of other campaigns in the past and present straightened
that out. We didn't want to come up with a pathetic, bloodthirsty campaign.

Furthermore, we were very disenchanted with the human race. Why are people who
know about the practices of the fur industry buying fur coats again? Why have models,
once featured on Peta-Posters, started to walk the world's catwalks wrapped up in
fox-skin again? Why are designers cutting fur again?

So, we kind of thought about a not so unrealistic scenario where all (wild/fur) animals
are extinct and people all of a sudden realize that something is missing. We thought
that people probably will start to build memorials for the unknown animal like they do
in post war eras. Pet Sematary anticipates this situation and hopefully helps to prevent
such a scenario.

How did you approach the look and tone of the site?
Leap of faith, time, feasibility, technology, the Ramones, Stephen King, and national
monuments are the ingredients primarily responsible for the appearance, texture,
and flavor of Pet Sematary. We basically mixed all ingredients together, preheated
the studio to 350 degrees, baked it in the team for three weeks, and then turned Pet
Sematary out and cooled it completely on a wire rack.

**While it's very simple, this site conveys a serious message without showing
any cruel images like many other animal right groups do. How did the client
react to this approach?**
First of all the client gave us a lot of creative freedom! Then, they followed our
recommendation to position Pet Sematary contrary to the campaigns of other animal
right groups and understood that we wouldn't need pictures at all. When seeing the
first dummy their reaction was more than positive!

DESIGNING A
HISTORY OF DESIGN

Second Story Interactive Studio creates a graphically arresting and meticulously organized archive for all of AIGA's past design winners. Split up by AIGA's "Year in Design" selections from last year and all other past winners, searches can be carried out by category or users can navigate selections by thumbnail.

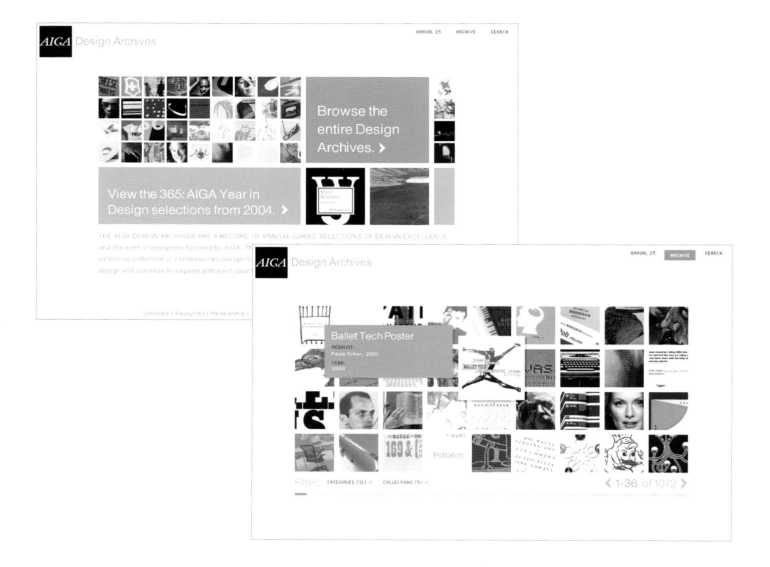

With such a client as AIGA, obviously the design and art direction of the site was of prime importance. Could you describe the considerations involved in the aesthetic of the site?

The Archive needed to be about the award-winning design projects. Of course, we had remarkable assets to work with. Visually, we wanted it to be minimal and unadorned, allowing the images to do the talking. This is not a site that should distract people with extraneous interface elements, bevels or drop shadows. Our goal was to give them an elegant, effortless interface that was straightforward yet engaging. The biggest challenge was to design an interface that can comfortably house anywhere from 5 to over 2000 thumbnails. The thumbnail gallery that we came up with is a great solution to the problem. It is truly expandable and flexible!

Agency
Second Story
Interactive Studios/Portland
Client
AIGA
Digital Artists/Mulitmedia
Carolyn Brewer, David Waingarten
Programmers
David Brewer, David Knape,
Thomas Wester
Content Strategists
Jeremy Clark, Marti Johnson
Designer
JD Hooge
Information Architect
Jeremy Clark
Creative Director
Brad Johnson
URL
designarchives.aiga.org/
Annual ID
05051N

The site is organized in two main veins: the design selections from the previous year and the archive of winning work from all previous years. What was your approach in organizing the profiled work?

A key goal of the site from the client's perspective was to maintain a way to feature the current year's winners in a more individualized fashion than the rest of the archive. We also wanted to give the current annual a similar yet more accessible format than the physical book that is sent out, so that visitors could visually "thumb" through the winners and single out designs that appeal to them. If the visitor selects an entry from the annual section, they are presented with a record screen that is the same screen they would see if they had come across the thumbnail for the same record in the Archive and selected it there. We also built the interface in such a way that AIGA can customize the color scheme and enter next year's winners using online database administration tools, providing a way to freshen the archive each year with a new batch of winners.

Can you explain how you approached the structure design of the site?

The Design Archives at launch contained winners, jurors and medalists from the past four years, but was designed and built to eventually support all records for all winners from the past 20 years and for many years to come. With this in mind, we knew that the interface would need to be flexible and allow visitors to easily filter the records by category and collection. The Archive section of the site accomplishes this with filters that can easily be toggled, and real-time seamless queries to the database, which happen without long delays or page refreshes. We also allow highly specific searches with the search interface, in which visitors interested in a particular format or topic can use the collapsible advanced search options, and further sort these results in the search results screens. Lastly we put the power of organization in the visitor's own hands with the light box feature. Simply dragging and dropping any image they see on the site down to the "light box" bookmarks it for easy retrieval, and the site also permits users to reorganize, edit and annotate their light boxes and then share them with others or view them as a slideshow. Our goal was to provide unfettered access to this excellent source of recognized design and inspire designers, students, professors, and clients alike, in an interface that is transparent and natural to use.

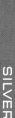

THE TRUTH
IS OUT THERE

With a content-rich site firmly planted in the grassroots vein, Crispin Porter + Bogusky and Arnold Worldwide ensure that youth have all the facts about Big Tabacco. The site features truth advertising campaigns, various downloads, 6 interactive games, the "rider report"—a journal from the road, and, perhaps most importantly, the real facts about smoking's effects on health and society.

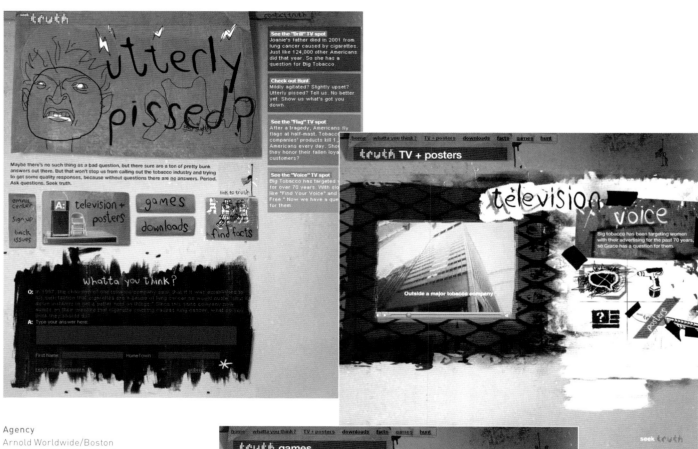

Agency
Arnold Worldwide/Boston
Crispin Porter + Bogusky/Miami
Client
American Legacy Foundation
Art Director
Meghan Siegal
Writer
Marc Einhorn
Programmers
Ebbey Mathew, Adam Buhler
Designers
Meghan Siegal, Chris Valencius,
Max Pfennighaus,
Suzanne McCarthy
Information Architect
Melissa Goldstein
Creative Directors
Ron Lawner, Pete Favat,
Alex Bogusky, John Kearse,
Tom Adams
URL
http://www.thetruth.com/
index.cfm?seek=truth
Annual ID
05052N

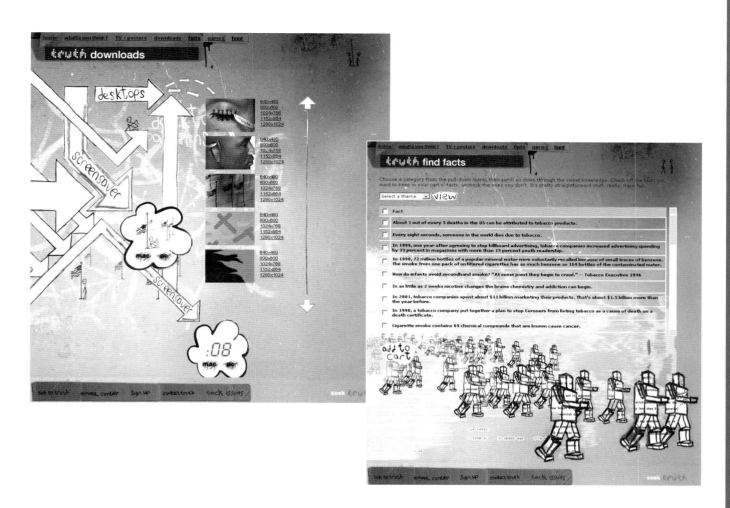

You clearly are targeting the youth market. Can you discuss the challenge of offering an alternative to the social forces and peer pressure kids face to smoke and getting them to visit the site?

The tobacco industry spends over $34 million every day marketing their deadly products. How can we appear as powerful as the tobacco companies? By using the one thing we do have that's more persuasive than fists full of money, and that's heads full of knowledge. Our first objective is to provide kids a dependable source of information to come to, to seek out the facts about the tobacco industry and get the tools they need to question this questionable industry for themselves.

We may have a little fun with the facts along the way, but we never add opinions or tell anyone what to do. You'll never get any of that "just say 'no' to cigarettes" stuff from us. So in the end, truth really is about making their own decisions based on knowledge and respecting the choices others make as well.

What was the thought process in organizing the different sections of the site?

Seek Truth comes out of the idea that there are a lot of unanswered questions surrounding the tobacco industry. So this site was designed to give kids the chance to easily express their own concerns and opinions about the tobacco industry and to provide a more specific platform for teens to ask questions and look for answers.

Each section of the site can be accessed through the initial landing page.

The page has a clear, modular layout from which all aspects are easily accessible. In one section, we offer up a variety of questions that kids can respond to and in turn raise questions of their own. Our photo blog provides users the chance to submit images of anything in their world, tobacco and non-tobacco related, that pisses them off. And by using the "fact cart" users can collect tobacco facts and create a custom pdf. As always, we provide, in a new and entertaining way, all of the downloads, commercials and games that those coming to our site expect to find.

WHEN HAIR
MEANS HOPE

In an execution laced with emotion and hope, OgilvyInteractive invites you to shave a former cancer patient's hair on behalf of cancer research for GRAACC.

Agency
OgilvyInteractive/São Paulo
Client
GRAACC
Art Director
Cassiano Saldanha
Writer
Moacyr Netto
Digital Artists/Mulitmedia
Felipe Mahalem, Andre Lima
Programmers
Vincent Maraschin,
Flavio Silva, Fernando Zomenhan
Content Strategist
Elaine Thompson
Designers
Felipe Lima,
Natalia Mazzacoratti
Information Architects
Leonardo Oliveira,
Rafael Taqueuchi
Creative Directors
Marco Antônio de Almeida,
Adriana Cury
URL
www.ourwork.com.br/hope
Annual ID
05053N

Shaving a kid's hair who has been a cancer patient is an emotionally touching experience. How did this concept come up?
Through providing a fun and gratifying experience by means of games and lighthearted activities, GRAACC manages to offer the children a balance to the difficult treatment of cancer, thus reducing future traumas.

Out biggest challenge was to convey this positive atmosphere. So we had the idea of showing a patient in a very delicate moment of the treatment: getting the hair shaved. The scene brought to the piece the tension we needed to approach the subject, touching people and making them interact. At the end of the piece, we reveal the kid has been cured.

What was the response from GRAACC?
GRAACC was very pleased. According to the hospital's marketing director, it was the piece created for them that most accomplished the task of conveying the essence of the work done by the hospital, with a strong, touching and positive message. During the time the piece was online, drive to GRAACC's site was 35% higher and the amount of donations increased 28%.

MAN IN THE MIRROR

OgilvyInteractive, utilizing impeccable morphing technology, showing a child age to a senior in the span of seconds, reminds us that volunteering time and money translates to saving lives.

DANIEL 4 YEARS OLD

DANIEL 12 YEARS OLD

DANIEL 22 YEARS OLD

DANIEL 47 YEARS OLD

DANIEL 70 YEARS OLD

The length
of my life
is up to you.

Did you get it?

GRAACC
Group of Support
to Adolescents and
Children with cancer

To donate or volunteer, click here.

Agency
OgilvyInteractive/
São Paulo
Client
GRAACC
Art Director
Pedro Gravena
Writer
Miguel Genovese
Content Strategist
Ilana Herzberg
Designer
Márcio Holanda
Creative Director
Marco Antônio de Almeida,
Paulo Sanna, Adriana Cury
URL
www.ourwork.com.br/morph
Annual ID
05054N

THE PEN IS MIGHTIER THAN THE SWORD

Meshing a long-time children's game with a deadly serious political message, Publicis Mojo stresses the importance of becoming a freedom writer for Amnesty International and potentially saving lives around the globe.

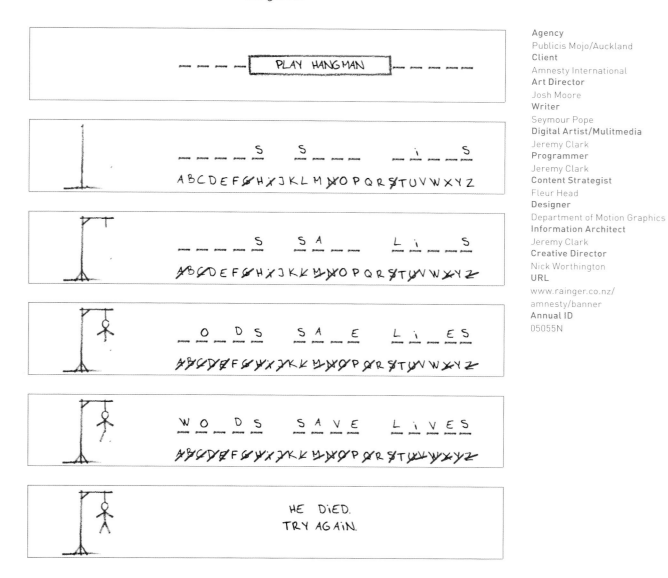

Agency
Publicis Mojo/Auckland
Client
Amnesty International
Art Director
Josh Moore
Writer
Seymour Pope
Digital Artist/Mulitmedia
Jeremy Clark
Programmer
Jeremy Clark
Content Strategist
Fleur Head
Designer
Department of Motion Graphics
Information Architect
Jeremy Clark
Creative Director
Nick Worthington
URL
www.rainger.co.nz/amnesty/banner
Annual ID
05055N

Taking the children's game "hangman" and applying it to the "Freedom Writer" Amnesty International campaign seems such a natural fit; a very simple and smart idea. Can you talk about the origins of the concept?

What's great about this ad is that the creative solution came in a dream. This has never happened before. Usually you think you've had a great idea in dream and you wake in the morning and they're terrible. I guess this is what happens when you become a little too obsessed with your work.

If you are unsuccessful at the game, the banner reads "He Died. Try Again." Was the decision to show that message a way to bolster the pay off of the game, "Words Save Lives. Become a Freedom Writer." and overall concept if you are successful?

It was a simple way of illustrating the result of not becoming a freedom writer in a manner which was intended to make the viewer begin to stop and think before they even reach the pay off.

MERIT WINNERS

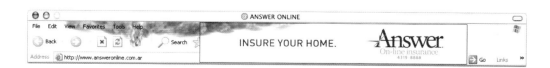

BANNERS . SINGLE

AGENCY
Dentsu/Tokyo
CLIENT
Sankyo

Art Director
Kaori Mochizuki
Writer
Takeshi Mizukawa
Digial Artist/Multimedia
Hiroki Nakamura
Designer
Kaori Mochizuki
Creative Director
Takeshi Mizukawa
URL
www.interactive-salaryman.com/
2004pieces/d0606e/
Annual ID
05077N

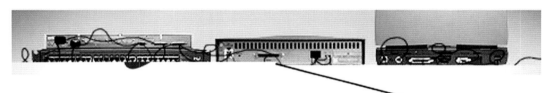

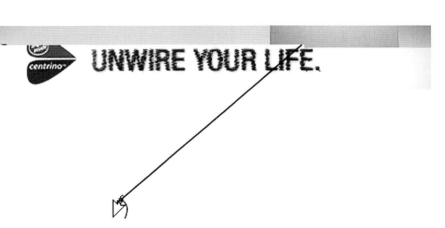

BANNERS . SINGLE

AGENCY
EURO RSCG 4D/São Paulo
CLIENT
Intel

Art Directors
Fabio Matiazzi, Rodrigo Buim,
Valter Klug
Writers
Ana Dolabela, Fabio Pierro,
Clovis La Pastina
Designers
André Castilho, Diorgenes Wenderly,
Lígia Ortiz, Lucía Silveira
Creative Directors
Alon Sochaczewski, Touche
URL
www.itsrainingagain.com/
english/24/
Annual ID
05068N

BANNERS . SINGLE

AGENCY
Freestyle Interactive/
San Francisco
CLIENT
EA

Art Director
Andrew Schmeling
Writer
Chris Gatewood
Programmer
Jezreel Alcantara
Designer
Amrafel Acosta
Creative Director
Andrew Schmeling
URL
confidential.freestyle
interactive.com/index.php
Username
oneshow
Password
winner
Annual ID
05071N

BANNERS . SINGLE

AGENCY
Goodby, Silverstein & Partners/
San Francisco
CLIENT
Hewlett-Packard

Writer
Peter Albores
Agency Producer
Amanda Kelso
Production Company
The Barbarian Group
Designer
Devin Sharkey
Creative Directors
Steve Simpson, Keith Anderson,
Will McGinness
URL
www.goodbysilverstein.com/
awards/banners/hp_zoom/
Annual ID
05062N

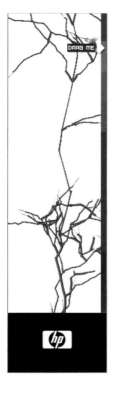

BANNERS . SINGLE

AGENCY
Goodby, Silverstein & Partners/
San Francisco
CLIENT
Hewlett-Packard

Art Directors
Will McGinness,
Dominic Goldman
Writer
John Matejczyk
Agency Producer
Mike Geiger
Production Company
Natzke Design
Creative Directors
Steve Simpson, Keith Anderson
URL
www.goodbysilverstein.com/
awards/banners/hp_vivera_
hummingbird/
Annual ID
05063N

BANNERS . SINGLE

AGENCY
Goodby, Silverstein & Partners/
San Francisco
CLIENT
Hewlett-Packard

Art Director
Will McGinness
Writer
Rick Condos
Agency Producer
Brit Charlebois
Production Company
Natzke Design
Creative Directors
Steve Simpson, Keith Anderson,
Will McGinness
URL
www.goodbysilverstein.com/
awards/banners/hp_timelapse/
Annual ID
05065N

AGENCY
Goodby, Silverstein & Partners/
San Francisco
CLIENT
Hewlett-Packard

Art Director
Will McGinness
Writer
Mike McKay
Agency Producers
Mike Geiger, Amanda Kelso
Production Company
Natzke Design
Creative Directors
Steve Simpson, Keith Anderson,
Will McGinness
URL
http://www.goodbysilverstein.com/
awards/banners/hp_vivera_blue/
Annual ID
05066N

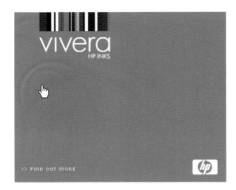
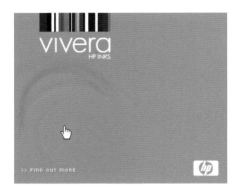
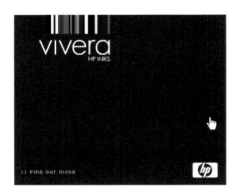

AGENCY
J. Walter Thompson/São Paulo
CLIENT
Ford

Art Director
Luiz Souza
Writer
Alessandra Muccillo
Digial Artist/Multimedia
Rogerio Nogueira
Programmer
Rogerio Nogueira
Designer
Luiz Souza
Creative Director
Suzana Apelbaum
URL
http://www.jwt.com.br/Awards_2005/
ecosport_offroad/en/
Annual ID
05069N

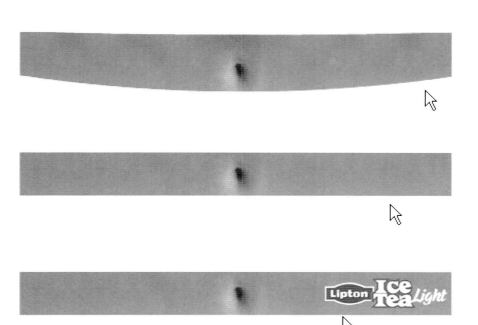

BANNERS . SINGLE

AGENCY
J. Walter Thompson/
São Paulo
CLIENT
Unilever

Art Director
Paulo Lemos
Writer
Paulo Lemos
Digial Artist/Multimedia
Rogerio Nogueira
Programmer
Rogerio Nogueira
Designer
Veni Cury
Creative Director
Suzana Apelbaum
URL
http://www.jwt.com.br/
Awards_2005/belly/en
Annual ID
05070N

BANNERS . SINGLE

AGENCY
TBWA\Santiago
Mangada Puno/Makati City
CLIENT
Caramba

Art Director
Louie Cale
Writer
Tanke Tankeko
Creative Director
Melvin Mangada
URL
http://tbwa-smp.com/
entries/hot.htm
Annual ID
05074N

AGENCY
TEQUILA\New York
CLIENT
ABSOLUT

Art Director
Lawrence Levene
Writer
Dave Keener
Programmer
Patrick Figueroa
Creative Director
John Bellina
URL
http://interact.tequila.com/
awards/absMakeover_com.html
Annual ID
05056N

AGENCY
Tribal DDB Australia/Sydney
CLIENT
Volkswagen Group Australia

Art Director
Murray Bransgrove
Writer
Giuliana De Felice
Designer
Mark Cracknell
Producer
Trevor Crossman
URL
www.tribalddb.com.au/
oneshow/volkswagen
Annual ID
05075N

REPLAY

Voted safest car ever tested in its class.
Euro NCAP 2004

BANNERS . SINGLE

AGENCY
Hakuhodo/Tokyo
CLIENT
World Wide Fund
for Nature Japan

Art Directors
Hiroaki Matsu, Yuji Suzuki
Writer
Toshiya Fukuda
Production Companies
TYO Interactive Design,
777 Interactive
Digial Artist/Multimedia
Yasuo Nihei
Designers
Yuji Suzuki, Shuhei Umene
Creative Directors
Toshiya Fukuda, Takayoshi Kishimoto
URL
http://www.tyo-id.co.jp/works/
banner/2004/wwf/01.html
Annual ID
05076N

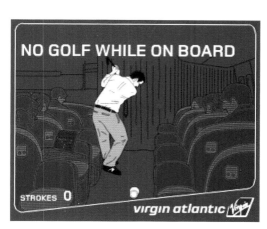

BANNERS . CAMPAIGN

AGENCY
Crispin Porter + Bogusky/Miami
CLIENT
Virgin

Art Director
Michael Ferrare
Writers
Franklin Tipton, Dustin Ballard,
David Gonzalez, Justin Kramm
Programmer
Juan-Carlos Morales
Production Company
The Barbarian Group
Designer
Rahul Panchal
Creative Directors
Alex Bogusky, Bill Wright,
Andrew Keller, Jeff Benjamin
URL
www.cpbgroup.com/awards/
bannersBoneshow.html
Annual ID
05079N
Also Awarded
Merit Awards: Banners . Single

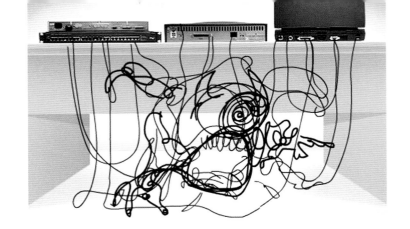

AGENCY
EURO RSCG 4D/São Paulo
CLIENT
Intel

Art Directors
Fabio Matiazzi, Rodrigo Buim,
Valter Klug, Rubens Miranda
Writers
Ana Dolabela, Fabio Pierro,
Clovis La Pastina
Content Strategist
Marcel Della Negra
Designers
André Castilho, Diorgenes Wenderly,
Lígia Ortiz, Lucía Silveira
Creative Directors
Alon Sochaczewski, Touche
URL
www.itsrainingagain.com/english/01
Annual ID
05081N

AGENCY
EURO RSCG 4D/São Paulo
CLIENT
Nokia

Art Directors
Fabio Matiazzi, Rodrigo Buim,
Valter Klug
Writers
Ana Dolabela, Fabio Pierro,
Clovis La Pastina
Designers
André Castilho,
Diorgenes Wenderly, Lígia Ortiz,
Lucía Silveira
Creative Directors
Alon Sochaczewski, Touche
URL
www.itsrainingagain.com/
english/14/
Annual ID
05082N

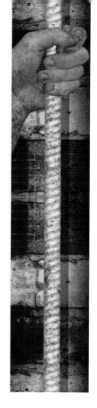

ROYAL MARINES
CHALLENGE

CLICK YOUR
MOUSE
REPEATEDLY
TO CLIMB
THE WALL

GOOD EFFORT BUT YOU ONLY HAD 100 METRES TO GO

BANNERS . CAMPAIGN

AGENCY
glue/London
CLIENT
Royal Marines

Art Directors
Christine Turner, Hayden Rogers
Writers
Simon Lloyd, Anne-Marie Burrows
Programmer
Simon Cam
Content Strategist
Martin Bailie
Designers
Leon Ostle, Dan Griffiths
Creative Director
Seb Royce
URL
www.gluelondon.com/
awards/2005/oneshow
Annual ID
05083N

BANNERS . CAMPAIGN

AGENCY
Goodby, Silverstein & Partners/
San Francisco
CLIENT
Hewlett-Packard

Art Directors
Yo Umeda, Sean Donahue,
Will McGinness
Writers
Aaron Griffiths, Rick Condos,
Peter Albores
Agency Producer
Mike Geiger
Production Companies
Natzke Design, The Barbarian Group
Creative Directors
Steve Simpson, Keith Anderson
URL
www.goodbysilverstein.com/
awards/campaign/hp_brand2/
Annual ID
05080N
Also Awarded
Merit Award: Banners . Single
(top image)

MERIT

BANNERS . CAMPAIGN

AGENCY
Lean Mean Fighting Machine/
London
CLIENT
AOL

Art Directors
Sam Ball, Dave Bedwood
Writers
Sam Ball, Dave Bedwood
Programmer
Dave Cox
Content Strategist
Tom Bazeley
Creative Directors
Sam Ball, Dave Bedwood
URL
www.lmfm.co.uk/
oneshow/aolchangeme
Annual ID
05085N

I bet you think I'm useless...

I can prove it. Just give me a chance!

Most people think of me as a dull banner,
but I'm just misunderstood

You're interested in what I can do
aren't you?

nod or
shake
your
mouse

HELP ME CHANGE! (COULD IF YOU ROLLED OVER ME)

now here
I can be a great banner with your help
AOL 9.0

BANNERS . CAMPAIGN

AGENCY
Lean Mean Fighting Machine/
London
CLIENT
Eyeblaster

Art Directors
Sam Ball, Dave Bedwood
Writers
Sam Ball, Dave Bedwood
Digial Artist/Multimedia
Specialmoves
Programmer
Dave Cox
Content Strategist
Tom Bazeley
Creative Directors
Sam Ball, Dave Bedwood
URL
www.lmfm.co.uk/oneshow/eyeblaster
Annual ID
05084N

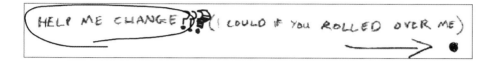
eyeblaster now has unlimited file size for your ideas.

eyeblaster (don't waste it.)

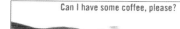
Can I have some coffee, please?

People with Parkinson's disease may not be able to do simple things.

But you can. Be patient.

Would you pass me the salt, please?

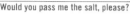

Can I have a toothpick, please?

BANNERS . CAMPAIGN

AGENCY
OgilvyInteractive Brazil/
São Paulo
CLIENT
Brazilian Parkinson Association

Art Director
Cassiano Saldanha
Writer
Moacyr Netto
Digial Artist/Multimedia
Felipe Mahalem
Programmers
Vincent Maraschin, Flavio Silva,
Fernando Zomenhan
Content Strategist
Andrea Tornovsky
Designer
Felipe Lima
Information Architects
Leonardo Oliveira, Rafael Taqueuchi
Creative Directors
Marco Antônio de Almeida,
Adriana Cury
URL
www.ourwork.com.br/patience
Annual ID
05086N

BANNERS . CAMPAIGN

AGENCY
Saatchi & Saatchi
New Zealand/Auckland
CLIENT
New Zealand Army

Art Directors
Brian Merrifield, Tom Eslinger
Writer
Matt Grainger
Digital Artists/Multimedia
Brian Merrifield, Tom Eslinger
Programmer
David Colquhoun
Content Strategists
Sarah Maclean, Nicola Harvey,
Heidi Tacbian, Lara Bowen
Designers
Tom Eslinger, Brian Merrifield
Creative Directors
Tom Eslinger, Brian Merrifield
URL
www.saatchinzonline.com/
f9banners_campaign
Annual ID
05087N
Also Awarded
Merit Award: Banners . Single
Merit Award: Brand Gaming . Banners

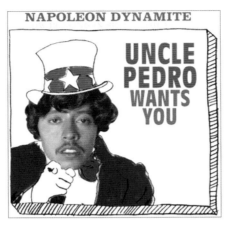

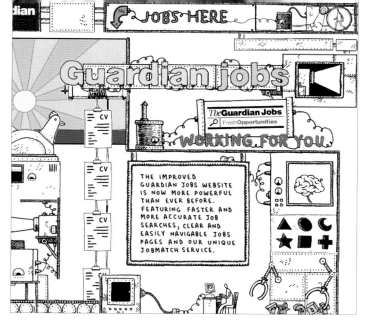

BANNERS . CAMPAIGN

AGENCY
Tribal DDB/London
CLIENT
Guardian

Art Director
Alex Braxton
Writers
Amy Gould, Ben Clapp
Digial Artist/Multimedia
James Robb
Designers
James Robb, Samantha Grant
Creative Director
Ben Clapp
URL
oneshow.concepts.tribalddb.co.uk/
Guardian/Jobs_Campaign/
Username
oneshow
Password
1show
Annual ID
05089N

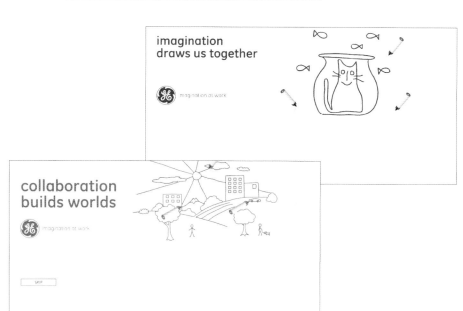

BEYOND THE BANNER . SINGLE

AGENCY
Atmosphere BBDO/New York
CLIENT
GE

Art Directors
Melissa Haworth, Ron Lent
Writer
John Heath
Digial Artist/Multimedia
Jeff Falcon
Producer
Mary Pratt
Information Architect
Ken Kraemer
Creative Directors
Andreas Combuechen, Arturo Aranda
URL
www.atmospherebbdo.com/awards/
2004/ge/imaginationcubed.htm
Annual ID
05090N

AGENCY
BEAM/Boston
Crispin Porter + Bogusky/Miami
CLIENT
MINI

Art Director
Jamie Bakum
Programmer
Alan Watts
Designers
Wing Ngan, Mike Ma, John Jackson,
T26 Fonts, House Industries
Information Architect
Marco Perucchi
Creative Directors
Birch Norton, Andrew Keller
URL
www.miniusa.com/crm/
load_mini.jsp?open=
custompaint&skip=yes
Annual ID
05091N

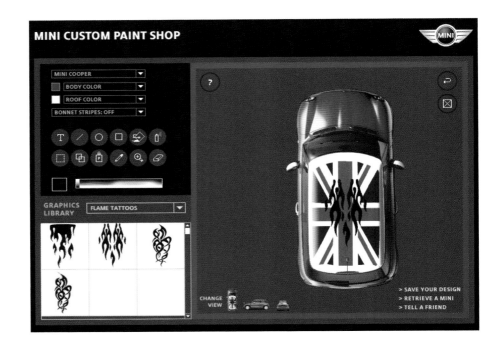

AGENCY
CP Comunicacion Proximity/Madrid
CLIENT
PUMA

Art Director
Eduardo Campuzano
Writers
Hugo Olivera, Guillermo Castilla
Programmer
Daniel Roig
Creative Director
Enric Nel-lo
URL
www.cp-interactive.com/
festivales/oneshow
Annual ID
05092N

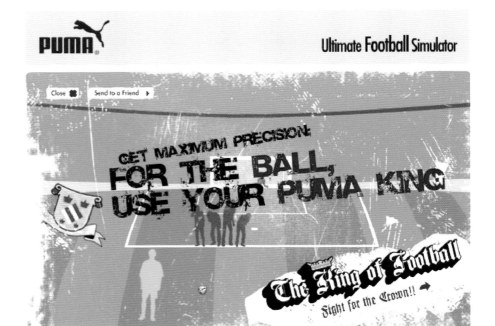

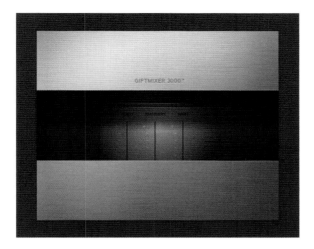

BEYOND THE BANNER . SINGLE

AGENCY
Crispin Porter + Bogusky/Miami
CLIENT
Borders

Art Directors
Joon Young Park, Michael Ferrare
Writer
Lydia Langford
Programmer
Robert Forras
Production Company
Firstborn
Creative Directors
Alex Bogusky, Tim Roper, Jeff Benjamin
URL
http://www.cpbgroup.com/
awards/giftmixer.html
Annual ID
05094N

BEYOND THE BANNER . SINGLE

AGENCY
Crispin Porter + Bogusky/Miami
CLIENT
Burger King

Art Director
Juan-Carlos Morales
Writers
Ryan Kutscher, Ronny Northrop
Programmer
Jason Soros
Creative Directors
Alex Bogusky, Andrew Keller,
Jeff Benjamin, Rob Reilly
URL
http://www.cpbgroup.com/awards/
ugoffliments.html
Annual ID
05095N

MERIT

AGENCY
Crispin Porter + Bogusky/Miami
CLIENT
Burger King

Art Director
Mark Taylor
Writer
Bob Cianfrone
Creative Directors
Alex Bogusky, Andrew Keller,
Jeff Benjamin, Rob Reilly
URL
www.cpbgroup.com/
awards/subservient_friend.html
Annual ID
05096N

BEYOND THE BANNER . SINGLE

AGENCY
Crispin Porter + Bogusky/Miami
CLIENT
Method

Art Director
Michael Ferrare
Writers
Bob Cianfrone, Paul Johnson, Dustin Ballard,
Jake Mikosh, Larry Corwin, Ronny Northrop,
David Gonzalez, Mike Howard, Brian Tierney,
Ryan Kutscher, Jackie Hathiramani,
Justin Kramm, Evan Fry
Photographer
Musilek
Programmers
Juan-Carlos Morales, Jason Soros
Production Company
The Barbarian Group
Designer
Rahul Panchal
Creative Directors
Alex Bogusky, Jeff Benjamin, Franklin Tipton
URL
www.cpbgroup.com/awards/
comeclean_scr.html
Annual ID
05093N

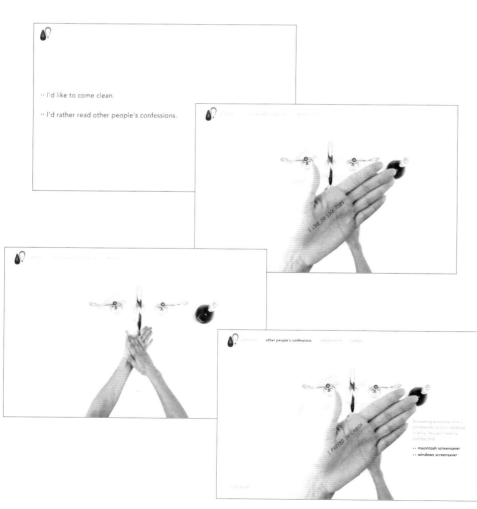

AGENCY
DDB Brasil/São Paulo
CLIENT
TAM Express

Art Director
Sergio Mugnaini
Writer
Fabio Victoria
Digial Artist/Multimedia
Raul Arantes
Programmer
Raul Arantes
Designers
Sergio Mugnaini, Raul Arantes
Creative Directors
Sergio Valente, Pedro Cappeletti,
Fernanda Romano
URL
www.dm9ddb.com.br/awards/
oneshow/testimonial.html
Annual ID
05097N

AGENCY
glue/London
CLIENT
Pot Noodle

Art Directors
Gemma Butler, Hayden Rogers
Writers
Seb Royce, Gavin Gordon-Rogers
Programmers
Simon Cam, Carl Huber
Content Strategist
Jerome Courtial
Designers
Dan Griffiths, Leon Ostle
Information Architect
Dan Griffiths
Creative Director
Seb Royce
URL
www.gluelondon.com/
awards/2005/oneshow
Annual ID
05099N

AGENCY
glue/London
CLIENT
Pot Noodle

Art Director
Hayden Rogers
Writer
Anne-Marie Burrows
Programmer
Simon Cam
Content Strategist
Martin Bailie
Designer
Simon Cam
Creative Director
Seb Royce
URL
www.gluelondon.com/awards/
2005/oneshow
Annual ID
05100N

AGENCY
Goodby, Silverstein & Partners/
San Francisco
CLIENT
Hewlett-Packard

Writer
Peter Albores
Agency Producer
Mike Geiger
Production Company
Unit 9
Creative Directors
Steve Simpson, Keith Anderson,
Will McGinness
URL
www.goodbysilverstein.com/
awards/holidaycards/festival.html
Annual ID
05098N

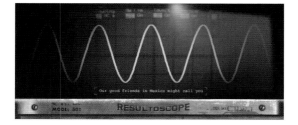

BEYOND THE BANNER . SINGLE

AGENCY
henderson bas/Toronto
CLIENT
Levi's Canada

Writer
Greg Bolton
Programmers
Scott Irwin, Neal Marques,
Norma Hislop
Content Strategists
Carolyn Convey, Laurie Del Bel,
Kathy Kohn
Designers
Colin Craig, David Wilson,
Shane Fleming, Phil Bonnell
Creative Director
henderson bas
URL
oneshow.hendersonbas.com
Annual ID
05101N

BEYOND THE BANNER . SINGLE

AGENCY
Modem Media/Norwalk
CLIENT
Hewlett-Packard

Art Director
John Jakubowski
Writer
Jenn Maer
Programmer
Dedric Reid
Content Strategists
Debbie Arora, Amanda Cox,
Lori Nowakowski
Designer
Dale Castro
Information Architect
Tina Pallitto
Creative Directors
Pat Phalon, Melanie Ferguson
URL
awards.modemmedia.com/
eno/05/oneshow/
Annual ID
05102N

MERIT

AGENCY
Saatchi & Saatchi Los Angeles/
Torrance
CLIENT
Toyota Motor Sales

Art Directors
Rahsaan Jackson, Scott Muckenthaler
Writers
John Bollow, John Diggins
Digial Artist/Multimedia
Marco Comparato
Producer
Allison Hoppe
Creative Directors
Steve Rabosky, Harvey Marco,
Scott Muckenthaler, John Diggins
URL
www.landcruiserheritage.com
Annual ID
05104N

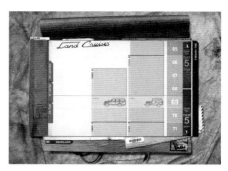

AGENCY
Daddy/Gothenburg
Springtime/Stockholm
CLIENT
ABSOLUT

Writers
Marika Jarislowsky, Open
Digital Artists/Multimedia
Magnus Oliv, Robert Melander,
Per Rundgren, Erik Sterner,
Daniel Pilsetnek
Agency Producers
Charlotta Larsson, Andreas Jerat,
Gustav Martner
Information Architect
Otto Giesenfeld
Creative Director
Björn Höglund
URL
www.absolut.com/raspberri
Annual ID
05105N

BEYOND THE BANNER . SINGLE

AGENCY
TAXI/Toronto
CLIENT
MINI Canada

Art Director
Danielle Krysa
Writer
Jason McCann
Programmer
Matt Burtch
Creative Director
Steve Mykolyn
URL
mini.ntrweb.com
Annual ID

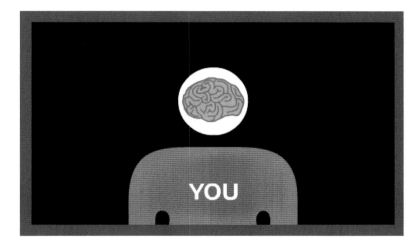

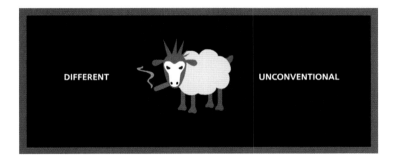

BEYOND THE BANNER . SINGLE

AGENCY
TAXI/Toronto
CLIENT
MINI Canada

Art Director
Paulette Bluhm
Writer
Jason McCann
Digital Artists/Multimedia
Andrew Harris, James Porter,
Graham Barton
Programmer
Pixel Pusher
Creative Director
Steve Mykolyn
URL
www.neverinneutral.com/
Black_Sheep/
Annual ID
05107N

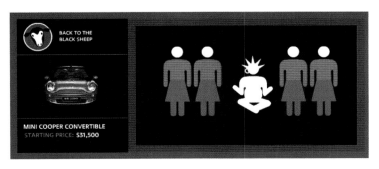

AGENCY
Zugara/Los Angeles
CLIENT
Reebok

URL
www.rbk.com/us/rbkstreets/
Annual ID
05108N

BEYOND THE BANNER . CAMPAIGN

AGENCY
Agency.com/London
CLIENT
Dulux

Art Directors
Adrian Peters, David Wellington
Writers
Adrian Peters, David Wellington,
Pavlos Themistocleous
Designers
Robert Mills, Dan Harman,
Karl Reynolds, Wil Bevan
Creative Director
Scott Bedford
URL
http://awards.london.
agency.com/chemistry/
Annual ID
05109N

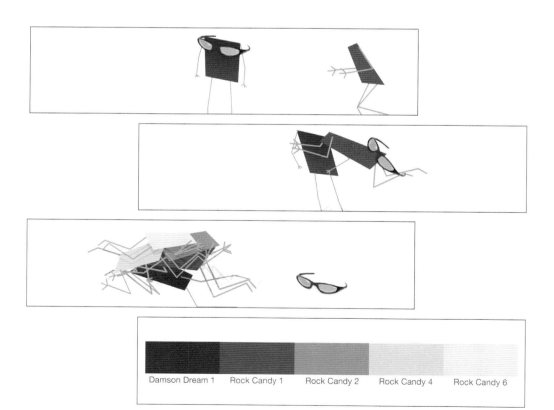

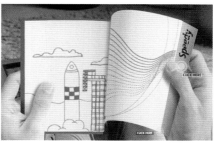

AGENCY
DDB Brasil/São Paulo
CLIENT
Telefonica/Speedy

Art Director
Sergio Mugnaini
Writer
Fabio Victoria
Digial Artist/Multimedia
Raul Arantes
Programmer
Raul Arantes
Designers
Sergio Mugnaini, Raul Arantes
Creative Directors
Sergio Valente, Pedro Cappeletti,
Fernanda Romano
URL
www.dm9ddb.com.br/awards/
oneshow/pocketbooks.html
Annual ID
05110N

AGENCY
Walt Disney Studios/Burbank
CLIENT
Walt Disney Studios

Writer
John Blas
Programmer
Trapeze, Avatar
Agency Producers
Susan Lambert, Justin Pertschuk
Producers
John Rito, Arnaldo D'Alfonso
Directors
John Blas, Arnaldo D'Alfonso
Creative Directors
John Blas, Federico Tio
URL
http://disney.go.com/disneypictures/
incredibles/firstinline/
Annual ID
05111N

MERIT

AGENCY
zentropy/Madrid
CLIENT
Volkswagen Spain

Art Director
Rodrigo Jatene
Writer
Pepa Rojo
Programmers
Fernando Reig, Raul Fernández
Content Strategist
Sebastián Méndez
Creative Director
Kuki Bastos
URL
www.be-on.com/2005/
oneshow/vw/polo/index.html
Annual ID
05112N

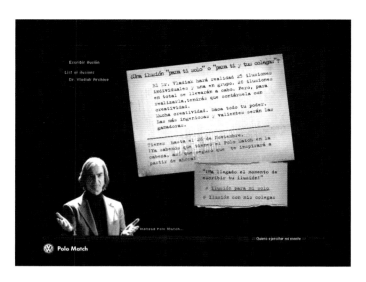

PROMOTIONAL ADVERTISING .
WEB SITES

AGENCY
180 Amsterdam (180\TBWA)/
Amsterdam
CLIENT
adidas International

Art Director
Dean Maryon
Writer
Richard Bullock
Digital Artists/Multimedia
Chris Bond, Darren Maryon
Programmer
Tom Wilde
Content Strategists
Darren Maryon, OD Consultancy
Designers
Chris Bond, Darren Maryon
Creative Directors
Richard Bullock, Dean Maryon
URL
www.odconsultancy.com/
impossiblejourney/
Annual ID
05113N

AGENCY
BEAM/Boston
CLIENT
PUMA + STARCK

Art Director
Carlos Lunetta
Digial Artist/Multimedia
James Cho
Programmer
Keith Peters
Creative Directors
Dave Batista, Birch Norton
URL
http://stage.beamland.com/
pumastarck
Username
puma
Password
oneshow
Annual ID
05114N

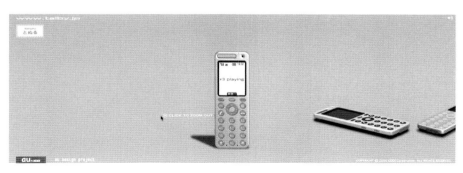

PROMOTIONAL ADVERTISING .
WEB SITES

AGENCY
Dentsu/Tokyo
CLIENT
KDDI

Art Director
Hirozumi Takakusaki
Writer
Nobuko Funaki
Digial Artist/Multimedia
Hiroki Nakamura
Programmer
Jun Kuriyama
Designer
Momoko Takaoka
Creative Directors
Nobuko Funaki, Hirozumi Takakusaki,
Hisayoshi Tohsaki
URL
www.interactive-salaryman.com/
pieces/talby_e/
Annual ID
05137N

PROMOTIONAL ADVERTISING .
WEB SITES

AGENCY
Dentsu/Tokyo
CLIENT
Nintendo

Art Directors
Hikaru Adachi, Seigo Nakano
Writer
Akane Hado
Digital Artists/Multimedia
Tomohiko Koyama, Yoshihiro Kojima
Programmers
Tomohiko Koyama, Masashi Ohashi
Content Strategists
Tadahisa Kido, Yukihiro Tominaga,
Junichi Uematsu
Designers
Kyosuke Taniguchi, Masakazu Okuda,
Masayuki Nishimura
Information Architects
Yusuke Tominaga, Shinya Fujiwara,
Toshi Matsushima
URL
http://nintendo.touch-ds.jp
Annual ID
05115N

PROMOTIONAL ADVERTISING .
WEB SITES

AGENCY
Dentsu/Tokyo
CLIENT
Toyota Motor Corporation

Art Directors
Rob Lindström, Yasuhito Imai
Digital Artists/Multimedia
Daniel Wallstrom, Simon Reeves,
Thomas Saeys
Programmers
Tetsuya Shintani, Masashi Matsukura,
Tetsuji Ooshita, Stefan Thomson,
Erik Eklund
Content Strategist
Akihito Abe
Designers
Yoko Otsuka, Charlotta Lundqvist
Creative Directors
Naoyuki Sato, Akihito Abe,
David Eriksson
URL
www.aoi-dc.com/classix/markx/
Annual ID
05138N

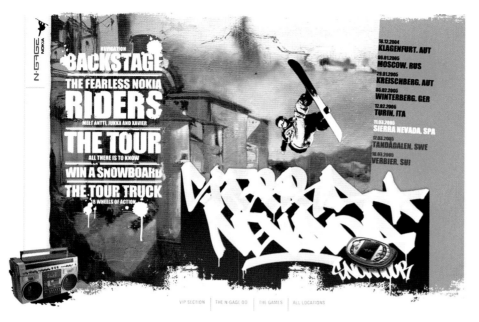

PROMOTIONAL ADVERTISING .
WEB SITES

AGENCY
Farfar/Stockholm
CLIENT
Nokia N-Gage

Art Director
Jakob Swedenborg
Writer
Henrik Berglöf
Digial Artist/Multimedia
Anders Gustavsson
Programmer
Bo Gustavsson
Content Strategists
Matias Palm Jensen, Emil Tavassoli
Designer
Fredrik Karlsson
Creative Director
Nicke Bergström
URL
http://www.farfar.se/
OneShow2005/snowtour
Annual ID
05118N

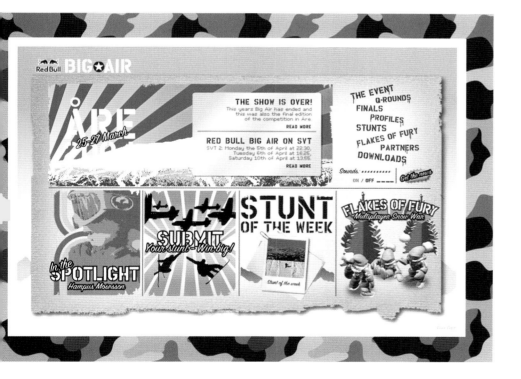

PROMOTIONAL ADVERTISING .
WEB SITES

AGENCY
Farfar/Stockholm
CLIENT
Red Bull

Art Director
Jakob Swedenborg
Digital Artist/Multimedia
Anders Gustavsson
Programmer
Bo Gustavsson
Content Strategists
Per Näsholm, Matias Palm Jensen
Designers
Erik Norin, Per Hansson, Tim Sajdak
Creative Director
Nicke Bergström
URL
http://www.farfar.se/
OneShow2005/redbull
Annual ID
05117N

PROMOTIONAL ADVERTISING .
WEB SITES

AGENCY
Firstborn/New York
CLIENT
Crispin Porter + Bogusky for Borders

Art Directors
Joon Young Park, Michael Ferrare
Writer
Lydia Langford
Digial Artist/Multimedia
Firstborn
Programmer
Robert Forras
Content Strategists
Paul Sutton, Ryan Thomas
Creative Directors
Alex Bogusky, Jeff Benjamin, Tim Roper
URL
www.firstbornmultimedia.com/giftmixer/
index.htm
Annual ID
05119N

PROMOTIONAL ADVERTISING .
WEB SITES

AGENCY
Framfab Denmark/
Copenhagen
CLIENT
Nike Europe

Art Director
Lars Cortsen
Writer
Rhiannon Davies
Programmer
Kim Jensen
Content Strategist
Bettina Sherain
Designer
Robert Thomsen
Information Architect
Peter Lau Hansen
Creative Director
Lars Cortsen
URL
framfab.dk/nike/speedsessions
Annual ID
05120N

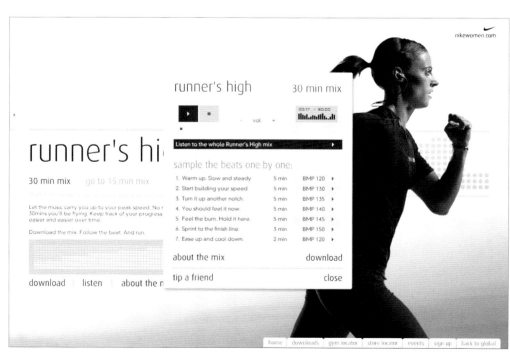
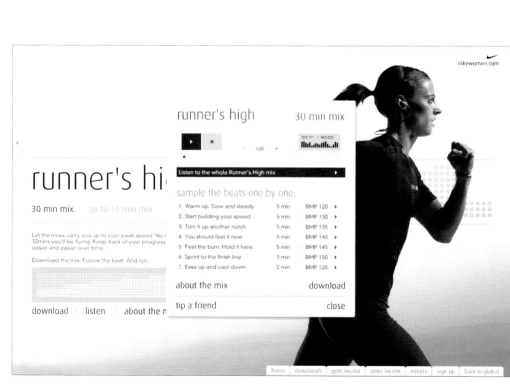

PROMOTIONAL ADVERTISING .
WEB SITES

AGENCY
Framfab Denmark/Copenhagen
CLIENT
Nike Europe

Art Director
Kamilla Blæsbjerg
Writer
Rhiannon Davies
Programmer
Philip Louderback
Content Strategist
Bettina Sherain
Designer
Peter Ringtved
Information Architect
Peter Lau Hansen
Creative Director
Lars Cortsen
URL
www.framfab.dk/nikewomen
Annual ID
05121N

PROMOTIONAL ADVERTISING .
WEB SITES

AGENCY
Framfab Denmark/Copenhagen
CLIENT
Nike Europe

Art Director
Rasmus Frandsen
Writer
Lewis Raven
Programmer
Jesper Arvidson
Content Strategist
Bettina Sherain
Designer
Tobias Prag Roesen
Information Architect
Jens Christiansen
Creative Director
Lars Bastholm
URL
www.nikefootball.com/ole
Annual ID
05122N

PROMOTIONAL ADVERTISING .
WEB SITES

AGENCY
Ground Zero/Los Angeles
CLIENT
Toyota

Art Director
Andre Fiorini
Writer
Tom O'Connor
Digial Artists/Multimedia
WDDG, Lobo
Programmer
WDDG
Content Strategists
Monique Veillette,
Anne Katherine Friis, Walter Harris
Designer
Andre Fiorini
Information Architect
WDDG
Creative Director
Court Crandall
URL
http://groundzero.net/putitinplay
Annual ID
05123N

PROMOTIONAL ADVERTISING .
WEB SITES

AGENCY
Herraiz Soto & Co/Barcelona
CLIENT
BMW

Art Director
Sergi Mula
Writer
Paula Mourenza
Digial Artist/Multimedia
Sergi Mula
Programmer
Carles Sanz
Creative Director
Rafa Soto
URL
www.herraizsoto.com/festivales/
bmwserie1micro
Annual ID
05124N

PROMOTIONAL ADVERTISING .
WEB SITES

AGENCY
Interone Worldwide/Hamburg
CLIENT
MINI

Art Director
Margit Schröder
Writer
Stephen James
Digital Artists/Multimedia
Hans Horn, Michael Ploj
Programmers
Kevin Breynck,
Lars Sonchocky-Helldorf
Content Strategist
Dirk Lanio
Designers
Silja Schulwitz, Stefan Schulz
Creative Directors
Martin Gassner, Oliver Bentz
URL
http://www.mini.com/
awards/cabrio_en
Annual ID
05125N

PROMOTIONAL ADVERTISING .
WEB SITES

AGENCY
Interone Worldwide/Hamburg
CLIENT
MINI

Art Directors
Antje Scholz, Meike Ufer
Writers
Stephen James, Jan Mattulat
Digital Artists/Multimedia
Michael Ploj, Andrew Sinn, Sven Loskil
Programmers
Kevin Breynck ,
Lars Sonchocky-Helldorf,
Rico Marquardt, Eva Sürek,
Nicole Kengyel, Oliver Rebbin,
Holger Knauer, Lutz Lonnemann
Content Strategists
Silke Gottschalck, Ulf Dieckmann,
Sven Schirmer, Anke Schliedermann
Designers
Silja Schulwitz, Stefan Schulz,
Margit Schröder, Tanja Fröhlich,
Olaf Boqwist, Nadine Schurr,
David Hoffmann
Information Architect
David Athey
Creative Director
Martin Gassner, Oliver Bentz
URL
www.mini.com/awards/cabrio_en/
Annual ID 05126N

AGENCY
Jung von Matt/Stuttgart
CLIENT
Neckar Valley Green Space
Foundation

Art Director
Stefan Walz
Writer
Oliver Flohrs
Programmer
Stefanie Welker
Designers
Stefan Walz, Fabian Bürgy
Creative Director
Achim Jäger
URL
www.am-neckar.de
Annual ID
05127N

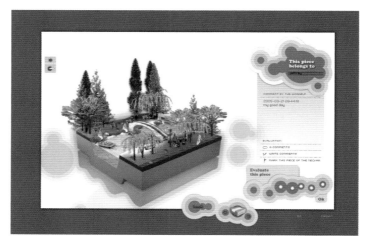

AGENCY
Lee Drasin/Universal City
CLIENT
Universal Pictures

Programmers
Arbel Meidav, Noah Gedrich
Content Strategists
Kevin Campbell (Universal Pictures),
Caren Lipson (Universal Pictures),
Kim Adams
Creative Director
Eric Perez
URL
www.twobrothersmovie.net
Annual ID
05128N

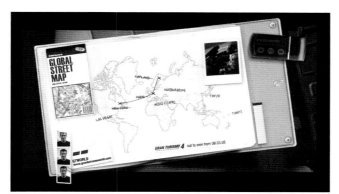

PROMOTIONAL ADVERTISING .
WEB SITES

AGENCY
Randommedia/London
CLIENT
Sony Computer
Entertainment Europe

Art Director
Darren Simpson
Writer
Jon Palmer
Programmer
Gordon Midwood
Designer
Xyn Xyu
Creative Director
Andy Sandoz
URL
www.granturismoworld.com
Annual ID
05130N

PROMOTIONAL ADVERTISING .
WEB SITES

AGENCY
Scholz & Volkmer/Wiesbaden
CLIENT
ThyssenKrupp

Art Director
Jörg Waldschütz
Writer
Judith Schütz
Digial Artists/Multimedia
Jörg Waldschütz, Elke Burhenne,
Constanze Fries, Jan Künzel,
Björn Pust, Patrick Jacobi
Programmers
Jens Schradin, Frank Langner,
Natascha Becker
Content Strategist
Judith Schütz
Creative Director
Heike Brockmann
URL
www.thyssenkrupp.com/discover
Annual ID
05131N

MERIT

PROMOTIONAL ADVERTISING .
WEB SITES

AGENCY
Daddy/Gothenburg
Springtime/Stockholm
CLIENT
V&S Absolut Spirits

Art Director
Jonas Hedeback
Writer
Frank Britt
Digial Artist/Multimedia
Mikael Forsberg
Programmer
Daniel Pilsetnek
Agency Producers
Gabriel Sundqvist, Charlotte Mörner Stein
Content Strategist
Gustav Martner
Designer
Erik Sterner
Information Architects
Per Rundgren, Otto Giesenfeld
Director
Patrik Persson
Creative Director
Björn Höglund
URL
www.levelvodka.com/overview
Annual ID
05132N

PROMOTIONAL ADVERTISING .
WEB SITES

AGENCY
Ted. Perez. + Associates/
Santa Monica
CLIENT
20th Century Fox

Art Director
Eric Perez
Writer
Taj Tedrow
Programmers
Michael Renninger, Noah Gedrich
Content Strategists
Liz Jones (20th Century Fox),
Damian Hagger (20th Century Fox),
Joe Feffer
Designer
Paul Hikiji
Creative Directors
Taj Tedrow, Eric Perez
URL
www.foxmovies.com/tdat
Annual ID
05133N

PROMOTIONAL ADVERTISING .
WEB SITES

AGENCY
Ted. Perez. + Associates/
Santa Monica
CLIENT
20th Century Fox

Writer
Taj Tedrow
Programmers
Arbel Meidav, Noah Gedrich,
Mike Kellogg
Content Strategists
Liz Jones (20th Century Fox),
Damian Hagger (20th Century Fox)
Creative Director
Taj Tedrow
URL
www.irobotnow.com
Annual ID
05134N

PROMOTIONAL ADVERTISING .
WEB SITES

AGENCY
The Upper Storey/Singapore
CLIENT
Nokia Corporation

Art Directors
Wayne Oi, Xavier Teo
Writer
Hemant Sampat
Digital Artists/Multimedia
Chye Yong Hock, Wayne Oi
Programmer
Pearl Chye
Content Strategist
Prakash Kamdar
Designer
Wayne Oi
Information Architect
Prakash Kamdar
Creative Director
Chye Yong Hock
URL
http://www.nokia7200le.com
Annual ID
05135N

PROMOTIONAL ADVERTISING .
WEB SITES

AGENCY
Wunderman/Chicago
CLIENT
Motorola

Art Directors
Dean Caruso, Rebecca Zdarsky
Writer
Rebecca Zdarsky
Programmer
Chad Rupp
Content Strategists
Mark Esbenshade, Rebecca Zdarsky
Designers
Dean Caruso, Chad Rupp
Creative Director
Michael Rezac
URL
http://www.motorola.com/ojo
Annual ID
05136N

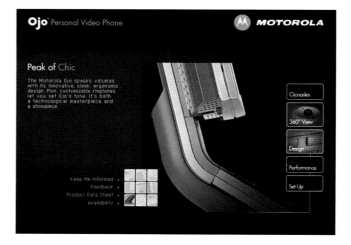

PROMOTIONAL ADVERTISING .
OTHER DIGITAL MEDIA

AGENCY
Forsman & Bodenfors/Gothenburg
CLIENT
Volvo Cars Corporation

Art Directors
Mathias Appelblad, Mikko Timonen,
Andreas Malm, Martin Cedergren,
Anders Eklind
Writers
Jacob Nelson, Filip Nilsson
Digital Artists/Multimedia
Kokokaka Entertainment,
Itiden, Astronaut, Stink
Designer
Jerry Wass
URL
http://demo.fb.se/e/volvo/
heartofvolvo
Annual ID
05139N

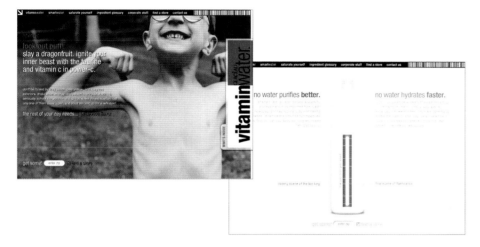

CORPORATE IMAGE B2C . WEB SITES

AGENCY
AKQA/San Francisco
CLIENT
Energy Brands

Digital Artists/Multimedia
Michael Powell, Nick Velloff
Content Strategist
Suellen Schlievert
Creative Directors
Brendan Dibona, Erik Rogstad
URL
www.vitaminwater.com
Annual ID
05140N

CORPORATE IMAGE B2C . WEB SITES

AGENCY
The Barbarian Group/Boston
CLIENT
KangaROOS

Art Directors
TOUCH, The Barbarian Group
Programmer
The Barbarian Group
Designer
The Barbarian Group
Creative Director
TOUCH
URL
www.kangaroosusa.com
Annual ID
05163N

CORPORATE IMAGE B2C . WEB SITES

AGENCY
BBmedia/Tokyo
CLIENT
Shiseido

Art Directors
Yoko Akimoto, Kouji Yamamoto
Writer
Shoko Yoshida
Programmer
Tatsuya Kido
Content Strategists
Takashi Nagoya, Masato Yoshikawa
Designer
Katsutoshi Araki, Rie Kitajima
Creative Directors
Kouji Yamamoto, Daisuke Hayakawa
URL
www.shiseido.co.jp/mj/
Annual ID
05141N

CORPORATE IMAGE B2C . WEB SITES

AGENCY
Blast Radius/Vancouver
CLIENT
Jordan Brand

Art Director
Marcus Ericsson
Programmers
David Cairns, Frank Budd,
Albert Liu, Bruce Pomeroy,
Andrew Archibold,
Byron Tredwell
Content Strategist
Greg Liburd
Producer
Jenny Winterbottom
Designers
Mitsuaki Yajima, Hannes Ottahal,
Ryan Massiah
Director
Amber Bezahler
Creative Director
Jon Maltby
URL
www.nike.com/jumpman23/
features/point5/index.jsp
Annual ID
05142N

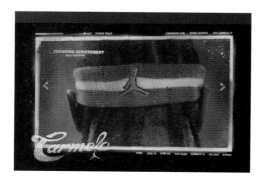

CORPORATE IMAGE B2C. WEB SITES

AGENCY
Business Architects/Tokyo
CLIENT
YAMAHA

Art Directors
Jun Yoshihara, Daizo Sato
Writer
Ikuko Noda
Digital Artists/Multimedia
Chika Kihara, Sadao Muraki,
Takayuki Nakahata
Programmers
Kazutoshi Shirai, Kyoko Suzuki,
Yukihisa Aoki, Shigeki Fujitani
Content Strategists
Kaoru Chono, Makoto Saito
Designers
Jun Yoshihara, Motoko Mizuno,
Kazuma Ito
Information Architect
Kaoru Chono
Creative Director
Ikuro Mine
URL
http://www.global.yamaha.com/
design/
Annual ID
05143N

Beautiful's New Cartel

Conspiring with your bloodstream to nurture skin where it starts, BORBA™ SKIN BALANCE WATER
and BORBA AQUA-LESS CRYSTALLINE are drinkable skincare, designed to smuggle
nutraceutical-packed microspheres to the deepest layers of dermis everywhere in your body.

Home   Product Overview   Skin Evaluator   Where to Buy   Our Philosophy   Register   Contact Us

CORPORATE IMAGE B2C . WEB SITES

AGENCY
Cole & Weber/Red Cell/Seattle
CLIENT
Borba

Art Director
Craig Erickson
Writer
Mike Tuton
Digial Artist/Multimedia
Todd Derksen
Programmer
Todd Derksen
Content Strategists
Brenda Narciso, Megan Eulberg
Designer
Craig Erickson
Information Architect
Carrie Vincent
Creative Directors
Guy Seese, Todd Derksen
URL
www.Borba.net
Annual ID
05161N

AGENCY
Cole & Weber/Red Cell/Seattle
CLIENT
Nike Team Sports

Art Directors
Craig Erickson, Todd Derksen
Writers
Kevin Thomson, Aaron Robnett
Digital Artists/Multimedia
Craig Erickson, Jeremiah Whitaker
Programmer
Roderick Stoelinga
Content Strategist
Steve Hawley
Designers
Craig Erickson, Jeremiah Whitaker
Information Architect
Carrie Vincent
Creative Directors
Guy Seese, Todd Derksen
URL
www.niketruefan.com/awards
Annual ID
05162N

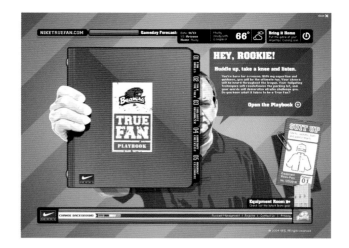

AGENCY
CP Comunicacion Proximity/Madrid
CLIENT
Volkswagen Audi España, S.A.

Art Director
Eduardo Campuzano
Writer
Hugo Olivera
Digital Artists/Multimedia
Sergio Garruta, Arturo Hernández
Programmer
Daniel Roig
Content Strategist
Alba Cristobal
Creative Director
Enric Nel-lo
URL
www.cp-interactive.com/
festivales/oneshow
Annual ID
05145N

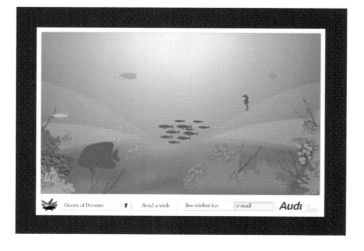

CORPORATE IMAGE B2C . WEB SITES

AGENCY
Crispin Porter + Bogusky/Miami
CLIENT
Burger King

Art Director
Juan-Carlos Morales
Writers
Ryan Kutscher, Ronny Northrop
Programmer
Jason Soros
Creative Directors
Alex Bogusky, Andrew Keller,
Jeff Benjamin, Rob Reilly
URL
http://www.cpbgroup.com/
awards/ugoff.html
Annual ID
05149N

CORPORATE IMAGE B2C . WEB SITES

AGENCY
Crispin Porter + Bogusky/Miami
CLIENT
Method

Art Director
Michael Ferrare
Writers
Bob Cianfrone, Paul Johnson,
Dustin Ballard, Jake Mikosh,
Larry Corwin, Ronny Northrop,
David Gonzalez, Mike Howard,
Brian Tierney, Ryan Kutscher,
Jackie Hathiramani,
Justin Kramm, Evan Fry
Photographer
Musilek
Programmers
Juan-Carlos Morales, Jason Soros
Production Company
The Barbarian Group
Designer
Rahul Panchal
Creative Directors
Alex Bogusky, Tim Roper,
Jeff Benjamin, Franklin Tipton
URL
http://www.cpbgroup.com/
awards/comeclean.html
Annual ID
05147N

CORPORATE IMAGE B2C . WEB SITES

AGENCY
Dentsu/Tokyo
CLIENT
NEC

Art Director
Yusuke Kitani
Writers
Naoyuki Sato, Satoshi Nakajima
Designer
Marcos Weskamp
Creative Directors
Naoyuki Sato, Satoshi Nakajima
URL
www.interactive-salaryman.com/
2004pieces/d0601e/
Annual ID
05168N

CORPORATE IMAGE B2C . WEB SITES

AGENCY
Firstborn/New York
CLIENT
Bacardi USA

Digial Artist/Multimedia
Gicheol Lee
Programmer
Dan LaCivita
Content Strategist
Jeremy Berg
Designer
Rita Lidji
Creative Director
Vas Sloutchevsky
URL
http://www.corzo.com
Annual ID
05150N

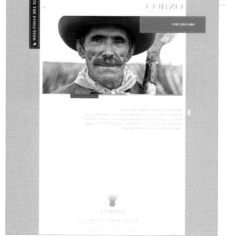

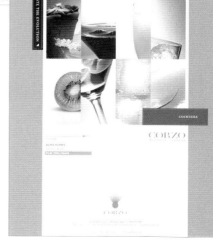

CORPORATE IMAGE B2C . WEB SITES

AGENCY
Fork Unstable Media Ost/Berlin
CLIENT
adidas-Salomon AG

Writer
Yvette Bradley
Digial Artist/Multimedia
Karsten Wiese
Programmer
Eduard Prats Molner
Designer
Christopher Nilsson
Creative Director
David Linderman
URL
www.adidas.com/com/tennis
Annual ID
05151N

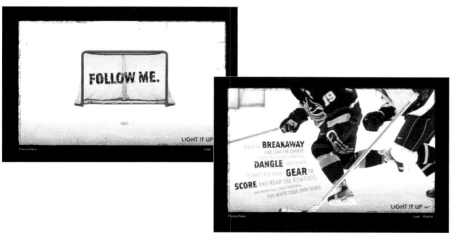

CORPORATE IMAGE B2C . WEB SITES

AGENCY
henderson bas/Toronto
CLIENT
Nike Canada

Writers
Jeff Reckseidler, Jon Finkelstein
Programmers
Norma Hislop, Suzanne Johnson,
Boris Pan, Guangde Wang,
Andrew White, Neal Marques
Content Strategists
Kathy Kohn, Jeff Reckseidler,
Duane Currie, Wes Schyngera
Designers
David Wilson, Phil Bonnell,
Paul McDougall, Stephen Bennett
Creative Director
henderson bas
URL
oneshow.hendersonbas.com
Annual ID
05152N

AGENCY
J. Walter Thompson Japan/Tokyo
CLIENT
Mazda Motor Corporation

Art Director
Hideki Owa
Writer
Akiko Yaeda
Digital Artists/Multimedia
Masaya Kato, Kenji Nanba
Programmer
Takashi Kamada
Content Strategist
Nobuaki Hongo
Designer
Hideki Owa
Information Architect
Yugo Nakamura
Creative Director
Yugo Nakamura
URL
www.jwt.co.jp/awards/mazda/
Username
awards
Password
jwt2005
Annual ID
05153N

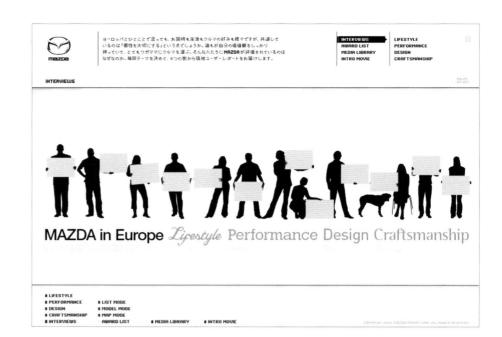

AGENCY
Kinetic/Singapore
CLIENT
Wong Coco

Art Director
Sean Lam
Writer
Alex Goh
Digital Artists/Multimedia
Sean Lam, Pann Lim,
Roy Poh, Victor Low
Programmer
Sean Lam
Designer
Sean Lam
Creative Director
Kinetic
URL
http://www.juicycubes.com
Annual ID
05154N

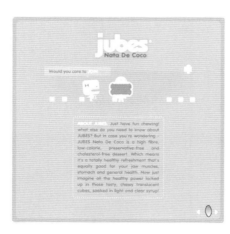

CORPORATE IMAGE B2C . WEB SITES

AGENCY
odopod/San Francisco
CLIENT
Nike

Art Director
Chris Brown
Writer
Kevin Imamura
Digital Artists/Multimedia
Sean Cronan, Ken Goto,
Trevor Graves, Michael Hernandez,
Jon Humphries, Todd Jordan,
Dennis Mcgrath, Gino Nave,
Chris Ortiz, Laura Plageman,
Giovanni Reda, Retrokid.com,
Scott Runcorn, Pixel Temple
Programmers
Ammon Haggerty, Gregory Cowley,
John Weir
Content Strategists
Jacquie Moss, Kevin Imamura
Designers
Chris Brown, Andre Andreev,
Ammon Haggerty, John Weir
Creative Directors
Jacquie Moss, Tim Barber, David Bliss
URL
http://www.nikeskateboarding.com
Annual ID
05155N

CORPORATE IMAGE B2C . WEB SITES

AGENCY
odopod/San Francisco
CLIENT
Nike

Art Directors
Tim Barber, Jess Ruefli
Writers
Tim Barber, Leighann Franson,
Tiffany Paul, Dennie Wendt
Digital Artists/Multimedia
Jason Martin, Rob Bruce,
Scott Runcorn, Marcus Swanson,
Bob Huff, Charles Chesnut,
Tim De Waele, Bill Cass, Tiffany Paul
Programmers
Ammon Haggerty, David Bliss
Content Strategists
Tiffany Paul, Margot Merrill
Designers
Jess Ruefli, Ammon Haggerty,
John Weir, Andre Andreev
Information Architect
David Bliss
Creative Directors
Tim Barber, David Bliss, Jacquie Moss
URL
http://www.nike.com/nikecycling
Annual ID
05156N

AGENCY
odopod/San Francisco
CLIENT
Red Bull

Art Director
Chris Brown
Writer
Tim Barber
Digital Artists/Multimedia
Ryder S. Booth, Alan Eldridge,
Bryan Medway, Jim Mutter, Gino Nave,
Christian Pondella, Scott Runcorn,
Jess Ruefli
Programmer
Michelangelo Capraro
Content Strategists
Rebecca Hill, Gwinn Appleby
Designer
Chris Brown
Creative Directors
Tim Barber, David Bliss, Jacquie Moss,
Kevin Townsend
URL
http://www.redbullcopilot.com/
Annual ID
05157N

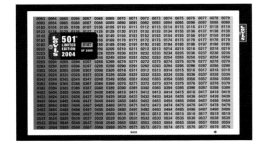

AGENCY
OgilvyOne/Singapore
CLIENT
Levi's

Art Director
Robert Davies
Writer
Peter Moss
Photographer
Roy Zhang
Programmers
Chandra Barathi,
Colin Foo, TV Raju
Producer
Memi Chang
Designer
Shawn Loo
Information Architect
Ben Galvin
Creative Director
Peter Moss, Dominic Goldman
URL
http://www.ap.levi.com/
livedin/index_a.html
Annual ID
05158N

CORPORATE IMAGE B2C . WEB SITES

AGENCY
R/GA/New York
CLIENT
Nike

Art Director
Chris Dowling
Writers
Scott Tufts, Jason Marks
Programmers
Charles Duncan, Nick Coronges,
Christine Reindl, Chuck Genco,
Todd Kovner
Content Strategist
Shawn Natko
Designers
Joseph Cartman, Mikhail Gervits
Information Architects
Yu-Ming Wu, Richard Ting
URL
http://awards.web.rga.com/
2004/bball.html
Annual ID
05159N

 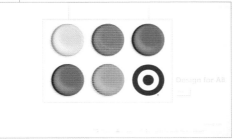

CORPORATE IMAGE B2C . WEB SITES

AGENCY
R/GA/New York
CLIENT
Target

Art Director
Andrew Clark
Writers
Paul Malmont, Melissa Bannon
Digital Artists/Multimedia
Ernest Rowe, Lian Chang, Dan LaPlaca
Programmers
Chris Hinkle, Tom Freudenheim
Content Strategists
Mae Flordeliza, Christopher Dugan
Designers
Piper Darley, Garry Waller,
Jeremiah Simpson, Karen Ngai
Information Architects
Cindy Jeffers, Diego Bauducco
Creative Directors
Kris Kiger, Ted Metcalfe
URL
http://target.com/
designforall/home.jhtml
Annual ID
05160N

AGENCY
Tokyo Great Visual/Tokyo
CLIENT
Daihatsu Motor

Art Director
Kengo Iizuka
Writer
Makoto Teramoto
Designers
Mika Takahashi, Akira Kumagai,
Fumihito Usukura, Hiwako Hamada,
Hiroki Nakamura
Creative Directors
Masataka Hosogane, Makoto Teramoto
URL
http://www.interactive-salaryman.
com/2004pieces/d0610E/index.html
Annual ID
05164N

CORPORATE IMAGE B2C . WEB SITES

AGENCY
Tribal DDB/London
CLIENT
Volkswagen

Writer
Ben Clapp
Digital Artists/Multimedia
Jamie Copeland, Ben Clapp,
Stephen Reed
Programmer
Jamie Copeland
Designers
Victoria Buchanan, Tim Vance,
Dieter Weichman
Information Architect
Chris Jenkins
Creative Directors
Ben Clapp, Stephen Reed
URL
www.volkswagen.co.uk/
gti/experience.html
Annual ID
05165N

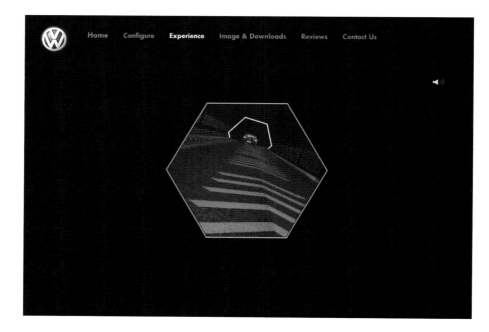

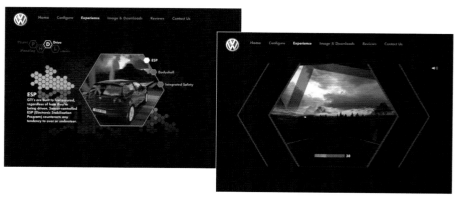

CORPORATE IMAGE B2C . WEB SITES

AGENCY
Wieden + Kennedy/Tokyo
CLIENT
W + K Tokyo Lab

Art Director
+CRUZ
Programmers
Shane Lester, Shojee Kukuchil,
Sunday Vision, Pedro Leon, Amauta
Designers
+CRUZ, WOOG, Shane Lester,
Shinsuke Koshio, Sunday Vision
Creative Directors
John C. Jay, Sumiko Sato
URL
www.wktokyolab.com
Annual ID
05166N

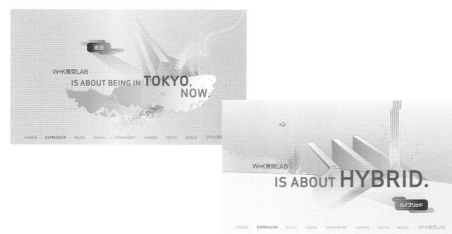

CORPORATE IMAGE B2C . WEB SITES

AGENCY
XM Asia Pacific/Singapore
CLIENT
Nokia

Art Director
Jeff Cheong
Programmer
Ronnie Liew
Designers
Danny Lim, Edwin Poh, Ong Sze Sze
Creative Director
Joseph Zandstra
URL
http://www.xm-folio.com/nokia/
entertainment/index.html
Annual ID
05167N

AGENCY
Zugara/Los Angeles
CLIENT
Reebok

URL
www.rbk.com/us/rbkstreets/
Annual ID
05169N

CORPORATE IMAGE B2C . WEB SITES

AGENCY
büro diffus/Stuttgart
CLIENT
Darius Ramazani Photography

Art Director
Martin Hesselmeier
Programmer
Uli Schöberl
Creative Directors
Holger Pfeifle, Christian Weisser
URL
www.ramazani.com
Annual ID
05216N

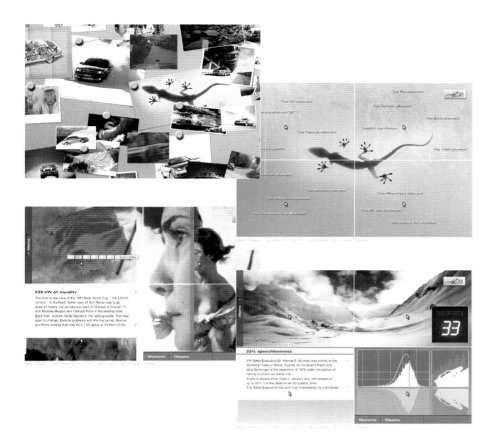

CORPORATE IMAGE B2C . WEB SITES

AGENCY
Elephant Seven GmbH Nord/
Hamburg
CLIENT
Audi AG Ingolstadt

Art Directors
Jan Hellberg, Elke Maasdorff
Writer
Alexandra Platz
Digial Artist/Multimedia
Matthias Harder
Programmers
Christian Koop, Alexander Funke,
Kim Christiansen
Designer
Tina Kläring
Information Architect
Rainer Sax
Creative Director
Oliver Viets, Dirk Ollmann
URL
http://bannertool.e-7.com/
awards 25quattro
Annual ID
05217N

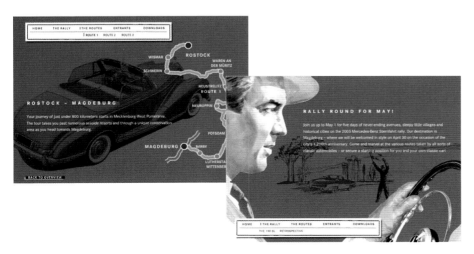

CORPORATE IMAGE B2C . WEB SITES

AGENCY
Elephant Seven GmbH Nord/
Hamburg
CLIENT
DaimlerChrysler
Vertriebsorganisation
Deutschland

Art Director
Kai Becker
Writer
Manfred Heider
Programmer
Christian Koop, Arne Otto
Designer
Till Warncke
Information Architect
Rainer Sax
Creative Directors
Dirk Ollmann, Daniel Richau
URL
http://bannertool.e-7.com/
awards/sternfahrt/
Annual ID
05218N

MERIT

CORPORATE IMAGE B2C . CD-ROMS

AGENCY
JWT Cheethambell/Manchester
CLIENT
Scruffs

Art Director
Tom Richards
Writer
Pete Armstrong
Creative Director
Andy Cheetham
Annual ID
05170N

CORPORATE IMAGE B2C .
OTHER DIGITAL MEDIA

AGENCY
Butler, Shine, Stern & Partners/
Sausalito
CLIENT
Converse

Art Directors
Robin Dafford, Charles Erdmann
Writers
Robin Dafford, Charles Erdmann
Designer
Tom Yaniv
Creative Directors
John Butler, Mike Shine
URL
staging.bssp.com/
oneshow_2005/converse/hoops
Annual ID
05172N

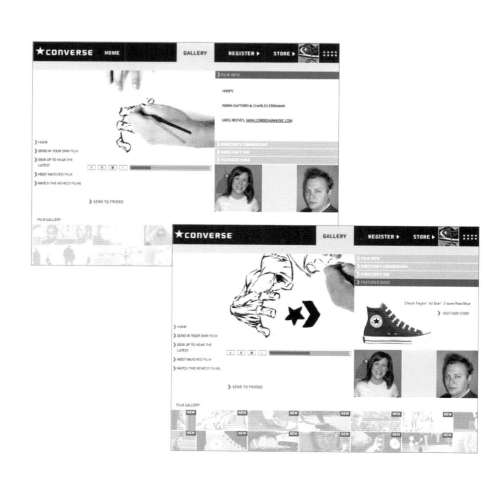

210   MERIT // CORPORATE IMAGE B2C . CD-ROMS & OTHER DIGITAL MEDIA

CORPORATE IMAGE B2C .
OTHER DIGITAL MEDIA

AGENCY
Bartle Bogle Hegarty/New York
CLIENT
Unilever

Art Director
Bill Moulton
Writer
Adam Reeves
Digial Artist/Multimedia
Matt Campbell
Programmer
Chris Berger
Information Architect
Chris Berger
Creative Director
William Gelner
URL
http://extranet.famefactorydigital.com
/work/AXE/feelmyyulelog/flash.html
Annual ID
05171N

AGENCY
Argonauten360/Dusseldorf
CLIENT
Grey Worldwide/Germany

Programmer
Oliver Rütgers
Creative Director
Chris Wallon
Annual ID
05173N

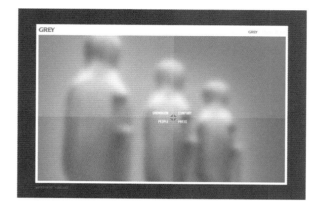

CORPORATE IMAGE B2B . WEB SITES

AGENCY
Goodby, Silverstein & Partners/
San Francisco
CLIENT
Diamond Nuts of California

Art Directors
Yo Umeda, Tanner Shea
Writers
Peter Albores, Jody Horn
Agency Producer
Victoria Brown
Production Company
WDDG
Creative Directors
Keith Anderson, Jon Soto
URL
www.goodbysilverstein.com/
awards/emeraldnuts/
Annual ID
05175N

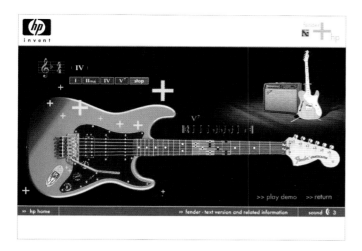

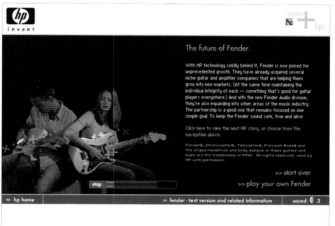

CORPORATE IMAGE B2B . WEB SITES

AGENCY
Goodby, Silverstein & Partners/
San Francisco
CLIENT
Hewlett-Packard

Art Director
Jeff Benjamin
Writer
Peter Albores
Agency Producer
Mike Geiger
Production Companies
Natzke Design, The Barbarian Group
Creative Directors
Steve Simpson, Keith Anderson
URL
http://www.goodbysilverstein.com/
awards/fender_experience/
Annual ID
05174N

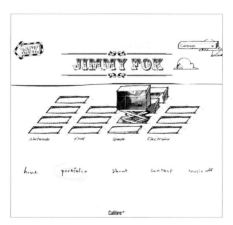

CORPORATE IMAGE B2B . WEB SITES

AGENCY
Kinetic/Singapore
CLIENT
Calibre

Art Director
Benjy Choo
Writer
Ken Choo
Illustrator
Benjy Choo
Digital Artist/Multimedia
Victor Low
Programmer
Benjy Choo
Designer
Benjy Choo
Creative Director
Kinetic
URL
www.calibrepics.com
Annual ID
05176N

E-COMMERCE WEB SITES . WEB B2C

AGENCY
Blast Radius/Vancouver
CLIENT
Jordan Brand

Art Directors
Marcus Ericsson, Francis Chan
Programmers
Rene Gourley, Terrance Yu,
Henry Leung, David Cairns, Brian Chen,
Alex Choi, Saleem Mahmood,
Rodrigo Gomez-Tagle, Ernie Bin,
Byron Tredwell, Bruce Pomeroy,
Steve Bond
Content Strategist
Greg Liburd
Designers
Tyler Payne, Mitsuaki Yajima,
Aimee Croteau, Christina Chu
Information Architect
Anthony Hempell, Amir Sharifnejad,
Jerome Valdez, Frank Budd,
Stacey Hung
Director
Amber Bezahler
Creative Directors
Mauro Alencar, Jon Maltby
URL
www.nike.com/jumpman23/
jordanxx/index.jsp
Annual ID
05177N

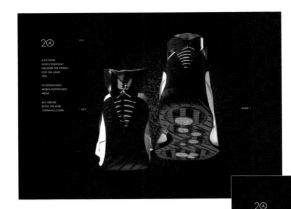

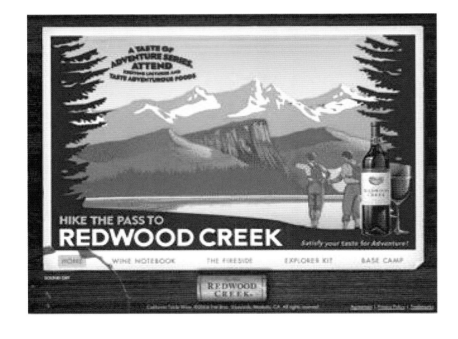

E-COMMERCE WEB SITES . B2C

AGENCY
EVB/San Francisco
CLIENT
Redwood Creek

Art Directors
Todd Bois, Heward Jue
Writer
Lisa Goodfriend
Digital Artists/Multimedia
Greg Roberts, Todd Bois
Programmers
Toby Boudreaux, Aaron Clinger,
Todd Bois
Content Strategist
EVB
Designers
Liz Balin, Jose Luis Martinez
Information Architect
Jason Zada
Creative Director
Jason Zada
URL
www.evb.com/enter_2004/
redwoodcreek.html
Annual ID
05178N

E-COMMERCE WEB SITES . B2C

AGENCY
Fallon/Minneapolis
CLIENT
Amazon.com

Art Director
Chris Wiggins
Writers
Eric Frost, David Carter, Greg Hahn,
Mike Smith, Christopher Toland,
Terry Rietta
Digital Artists/Multimedia
Andy Gugel, Andy Lemay
Programmer
Andy Lemay
Agency Producers
Jules Daly, Brian DiLorenzo,
Fran McGivern, Marjie-Brian DiLorenzo
Producers
Jules Daly, Fran McGivern,
Marjie Abrahams
Content Strategist
Chris Wiggins
Production Company
RSA USA, Inc.
Designer
Andy Gugel
Information Architect
Chris Wiggins
Directors
Acne, Jake Scott, Tony Scott,
David Slade, Jordan Scott
Creative Directors
Kevin Flatt, Chris Wiggins, David Lubars
URL
awards.fallon.com/index.aspx?pro=200
Annual ID 05179N

E-COMMERCE WEB SITES . B2C

AGENCY
Periscope/Minneapolis
CLIENT
Caribou Coffee

Art Director
Gordon Lee
Writers
Katerina Martchouk, Kerry Casey
Digial Artist/Multimedia
Greg Schomburg
Programmer
Adam Knutson
Content Strategist
Katerina Martchouk
Designer
Brad Schueth
Information Architects
Klay DeVries, Casey Quinn
Creative Directors
Chris Cortilet, Kerry Casey
URL oneshow.periscope.com
Username oneshow0105
Password interactive
Annual ID 05180N

AGENCY
R/GA/New York
CLIENT
Nike

Art Director
Marlon Hernandez
Writers
Josh Bletterman, Scott Tufts
Programmers
Scott Prindle, Sean Lyons,
Chuck Genco, Stan Wiechers,
Martin Legowiecki
Content Strategists
Winston Binch, Matt Howell
Designers
Ian Brewer, David Hyung
Information Architects
Matt Walsh, Richard Ting
URL
http://awards.web.rga.com/2004/
nike_id.html
Annual ID
05181N

E-COMMERCE WEB SITES . B2C

AGENCY
R/GA/New York
CLIENT
Nike

Art Director
Jerome Austria
Writers
Josh Bletterman, Jamie McPhee,
Thomas Pettus
Digial Artist/Multimedia
Len Toomey
Programmers
Christine Reindl, Noel Billig,
Stuart Buchbinder, Scott Prindle
Content Strategists
Jennifer Allen, Paul Maingot
Designers
Johanna Langford, Mini Ham,
Phil Lubliner
Information Architect
Aya Karpinska
URL
http://awards.web.rga.com/2004/
women.html
Annual ID
05182N

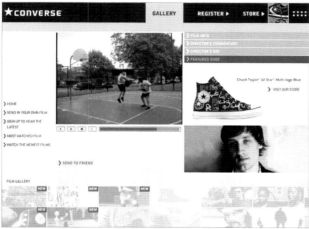

E-COMMERCE . OTHER DIGITAL MEDIA

AGENCY
Butler, Shine, Stern & Partners/
Sausalito
CLIENT
Converse

Art Director
Mike Hughes
Writer
Mike Hughes
Designer
Tom Yaniv
Creative Directors
John Butler, Mike Shine
URL
http://staging.bssp.com/
oneshow_2005/
converse/revolutions
Annual ID
05183N

E-COMMERCE . OTHER DIGITAL MEDIA

AGENCY
Butler, Shine, Stern & Partners/
Sausalito
CLIENT
Converse

Art Director
Harry Bliss
Writer
Harry Bliss
Designer
Tom Yaniv
Creative Directors
John Butler, Mike Shine
URL
http://staging.bssp.com/
oneshow_2005/converse/
hold_the_phone/
Annual ID
05184N

INTEGRATED BRANDING CAMPAIGN

AGENCY
Bensimon Byrne/Toronto
CLIENT
Ministry of Health
and Long Term Care

Art Directors
Mark Spalding, Anthony DelRizzo
Writers Chris Munnik, Trish Kavanagh,
Maggie Screaton
Illustrator
Geoff Donovan
Digital Artists/Multimedia
Anthony DelRizzo, Geoff Donovan,
Darren Donovan
Programmers
JJ Sullivan, Steve Headley,
Jonathan Sanford,
Marc Aucoin
Agency Producer
Johnny Chambers
Content Strategist
Cameron Wykes
Production Company
Directors Film
Designer Anthony DelRizzo
Director James Haworth
Creative Directors
David Rosenberg, Cameron Wykes
URL www.stupid.ca
Annual ID 05185N
Also Awarded
Merit Award: Non-Profit . Web Sites

INTEGRATED BRANDING CAMPAIGN

AGENCY
BEAM/Boston
Crispin Porter + Bogusky/Miami
CLIENT
MINI

Art Directors Paul Keister,
Jed Grossman, Jamie Bakum
Writers Bob Cianfrone, Bill Wright,
David Povill, Birch Norton
Photographers Zach Gold, Jamie Bakum,
Sebastian Gray, Peter Hetzmannseder
Illustrators Mike Wislocki, Andrew King,
Marc Leuchner (animation)
Digital Artist/Multimedia Mike Wislocki
Programmers Mike Wislocki, Sam Roach,
Juan-Carlos Morales
Agency Producers Rupert Samuel,
Teri Vasarhelyi, Paul Sutton,
Julieana Stechschulte, Sebastian Gray
Production Company
HSI/New York, Los Angeles
Designer Emily Taylor
Director Gerard de Thame
Creative Directors Alex Bogusky,
Dave Batista, Andrew Keller, Birch Norton,
Jeff Benjamin, Steve O'Connell
URL http://www.cpbgroup.com/
awards/jump_int.html
Annual ID 05186N

INTEGRATED BRANDING CAMPAIGN

AGENCY
Digitas/New York
Ogilvy & Mather/New York
CLIENT
American Express

Art Directors
Nick Barrios, Frank Guzzone
Writers Atit Shah,
Christian Charles, Stewart Krull
Photographers
David Jacquot, Gary Owens
Illustrator DC Comics
Digital Artists/Multimedia
WDDG, @radical.media
Programmers WDDG, John Young
Agency Producers Elyse Rubin,
Cheryl Gackstetter, Texas East
Content Strategists
Daniela Gennaoui, Nadja Bellan-White
Production Companies
WDDG, @radical.media, The Spotty Dog
Designer Nick Barrios
Information Architects
Nick Barrios, Billy Seabrook
Director Barry Levinson
Creative Directors Mark Beeching,
Matt D'Ercole, David Apicella,
Chris Mitton, Billy Seabrook
URL http://nycpresentations.digitas.
com/digitas_ny__awards/seinfeld
Username Digitas
Password @w@rds
Annual ID 05187N

INTEGRATED BRANDING CAMPAIGN

AGENCY
Fallon/New York
Fallon Interactive/Minneapolis
CLIENT
Virgin Mobile USA

Art Directors Wayne Best,
Marcus Woolcott, Paul Bichler
Writer Adam Alshin
Illustrators Fiona Hewitt, David Annis
Digial Artist/Multimedia Dan Boen
Programmers
Jason Streigal, Dan Boen
Agency Producers Zarina Mak,
Louise Doherty, Michelle Domeyer
Production Company MJZ
Designers Paul Bichler, Kim Haxton
Information Architect Mark Hines
Directors Tom Kuntz, Mike Maguire
Creative Directors
Ari Merkin, Kevin Flatt,
Paul Bichler, Wayne Best
URL http://awards.fallon.com/index.
aspx?camp=24
Annual ID 05188N
Also Awarded
Merit Award:
Promotional Advertising . Web Sites

INTEGRATED BRANDING CAMPAIGN

AGENCY
Forsman & Bodenfors/
Gothenburg
CLIENT
Abba Seafood

Art Directors
Martin Cedergren, Joakim Blondell
Writer
Martin Ringqvist
Digial Artist/Multimedia
Daddy
Agency Producer
Mathias Appelblad
Annual ID
05190N

INTEGRATED BRANDING CAMPAIGN

AGENCY
Forsman & Bodenfors/
Gothenburg
CLIENT
Volvo Cars Sweden/Volvo V50

Art Directors
Martin Cedergren, Mikko Timonen,
Anders Eklind
Writers
Filip Nilsson, Jacob Nelson
Photographer
Peter Gherke
Agency Producer
Mathias Appelblad
Production Company
Kokokaka Entertainment
Designer
Jerry Wass
URL
http://demo.fb.se/e/v50/
Annual ID
05189N

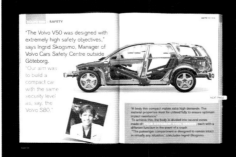

INTEGRATED BRANDING CAMPAIGN

AGENCY
Fuel Europe/Amsterdam
CLIENT
Volvo Cars Corporation

Art Directors
Vivian Walsh, Bertrand Fleuret
Writer
Lorenzo De Rita
Photographer
Jason Fulford
Digial Artists/Multimedia
EHS Brann, Marc Williams,
Matt Page, Gavin King, John Hatfield,
Tom Hedstrom, Sharon Green
Agency Producers
Dave Evans, Nils Schwemer,
Chayenne de Witte
Production Companies
MJZ, Quad Productions,
@radical.media
Directors
Lance Bangs, Remy Belvaux,
Roman Coppola
Creative Director
Lorenzo De Rita
URL
www.volvocars.co.uk/_campaigns/
LifeOnBoard/
Annual ID
05191N

INTEGRATED BRANDING CAMPAIGN

AGENCY
McKinney/Durham
CLIENT
Audi of America

Art Directors
Bruce Fougere, Dino Valentini
Writers
Bruce Fougere, Lara Bridger
Photographer
Mark Seliger
Digial Artist/Multimedia
Kelly Cooper
Programmer
Robb Hamilton
Agency Producers
Regina Brizzolara, Lisa Kirkpatrick
Content Strategist
Erin Bredemann
Production Company
Park Pictures
Designers
Eric Connor, Kelly Cooper
Director
Lance Acord
Creative Directors
David Baldwin, Dave Cook,
Jonathan Cude, Bruce Fougere
Annual ID
05192N

INTEGRATED BRANDING CAMPAIGN

AGENCY
OgilvyOne/New York
CLIENT
Dove

Art Directors
Sabine Grammersdorf,
Bill Bonomo
Writers
Kim Mathers, Lori Dudek,
Aurelio Saiz, Christine Montaquila
Photographer
Ian Rankin
Programmers
Guy Shahar, Livern Chin,
John McGeehan, Irwin Horowitz
Agency Producers
Eric Ayala, Terri Dannenberg
Creative Directors
Steve Hayden, Jan Leth, Bruce Lee,
Dennis Lewis, Aurelio Saiz,
Bill Bonomo
URL
www.wwpl.net/OneShow2005/
dove.html
Annual ID
05193N

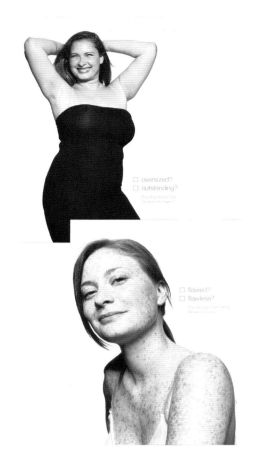

INTEGRATED BRANDING CAMPAIGN

AGENCY
OgilvyOne/New York
CLIENT
IBM

Art Directors
Alastair Green, Kellie Kalvig
Writers
Simon Foster, Mark Emerson, John Park
Programmers
Yefim Krasnyanskiy, John McGeehan,
Peter Ng, Ernie Parada,
Jonathan Schnapps, Todd Yard,
Drew Ziegler, Julia Jia
Agency Producers
Terri Dannenberg, Dana Edelman,
John Gossimer, Jeremy Saulnier,
Lee Weiss, Raul Aristud, Chrsitopher Zobel
Designers
Bill Bergman, Kerry Goeller,
Nicole O'Donnell, Jill Ruckelshaus,
Dan Williams
Creative Directors
Jan Leth, Chris Wall, Greg Kaplan,
Tom Bagot, Rob Bagot, Tom Godici
URL
www.wwpl.net/OneShow2005/
ibm/index.html
Annual ID 05194N
Also Awarded
Merit Award: Banners . Single

INTEGRATED BRANDING CAMPAIGN

AGENCY
Publicis Mojo/Melbourne
CLIENT
Nike

Art Directors
Tanya Michaelides, David Klein
Writers
Michelle Withers, Steve Jackson
Photographer
Chris Von Menge
Digial Artist/Multimedia &
Programmer Volume
Agency Producers
Sally McLennan, Corey Esse
Production Companies
Volume, Exit Films
Designer Mark Molloy
Information Architects
Publicis Mojo, Volume
Director Mark Molloy
Creative Director Darren Spiller
URL http://www.volume.net.au/
publicismojo/index.cfm
Username publicis
Password Pub05awa
Annual ID 05195N
Also Awarded
Merit Award:
Promotional Advertising . Web Sites

INTEGRATED BRANDING CAMPAIGN

AGENCY
Wieden + Kennedy/New York
CLIENT
SHARP Aquos

Art Directors
Alan Buchanan, Stuart Jennings
Writer Andy Carrigan
Digial Artist/Multimedia
TOMATO
Agency Producers
Gary Krieg, Temma Shoaf,
Jesse Wann, Katie Shields
Content Strategists
Jennifer Colman, Andy Carrigan
Production Companies
Villains, @radical.media,
Chelsea Pictures,
Haxan Entertainment, GMD Studios
Designer TOMATO
Information Architect Jon Zast
Directors
Philippe Andre, Errol Morris
Creative Directors
Todd Waterbury, Ty Montague,
John C. Jay, Sumiko Sato
URL www.moretosee.com
Annual ID 05196N

BRAND GAMING . BANNERS

AGENCY
Big Spaceship/Brooklyn
CLIENT
20th Century Fox

Art Director
D. Garrett Nantz
Digial Artist/Multimedia
David Chau
Programmer
Joshua Hirsch
Designers
David Chau, Peter Reid,
Tyson Damman, George Murray
Creative Director
Daniel Federman
URL
www.bigspaceship.com/
oneshow/avp/
Annual ID
05197N

BRAND GAMING . BANNERS

AGENCY
Tribal DDB/London
CLIENT
Guardian

Writers
Liam Casey, David Partington
Digial Artist/Multimedia
James Newman
Programmer
James Newman
Designer
James Newman
Information Architect
Chris Jenkins
Creative Directors
Ben Clapp, Stephen Reed
URL
oneshow.concepts.tribalddb.
co.uk Guardian/Ryder_Cup/
ryder_468x60tz.swf.html
Username
oneshow
Password
1show
Annual ID
05199N

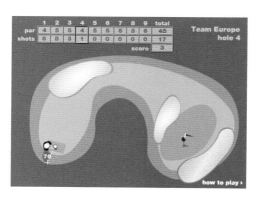

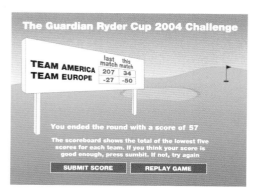

BRAND GAMING . WEB SITES

AGENCY
AlmapBBDO/São Paulo
CLIENT
Effen

Art Director
Adhemas Batista
Writers
Bruno Godinho, Rodolfo Barreto
Programmers
Guiherme Cavallini, Fabio Toledo,
Marcos Roque
Designer
Haydee Uekubo
Creative Directors
Marcello Serpa, Rodrigo Almeida
URL
www.almapbbdo.com.br/
awards/2005/effen/twix
Annual ID
05200N

visit www.GotUsed.com for more games and cool prizes.

BRAND GAMING . WEB SITES

AGENCY
Archrival/Lincoln
CLIENT
Nebraska Book Company

Art Director
Cass Kovanda
Digital Artists/Multimedia
Cass Kovanda, Bart Johnston
Programmer
Bart Johnston
Content Strategist
Joe Goddard
Designers
Cass Kovanda, Bart Johnston
Information Architect
Joe Goddard
URL
www.gotused.com/games/poom/
Annual ID
05201N

AGENCY
BEAM/Boston
Crispin Porter + Bogusky/Miami
CLIENT
MINI

Art Directors
Jed Grossman, Jamie Bakum
Writers
David Povill, Birch Norton
Digital Artists/Multimedia
Mike Wislocki, Andrew King,
Marc Leuchner (animation)
Programmers
Mike Wislocki, Sam Roach
Designer
Emily Taylor
Creative Directors
Alex Bogusky, Dave Batista,
Andrew Keller, Birch Norton,
Jeff Benjamin, Steve O'Connell
URL
www.cpbgroup.com/
awards/jump.html
Annual ID
05204N

AGENCY
Big Spaceship/Brooklyn
CLIENT
Universal Pictures

Art Director
David Chau
Writer
Drew Horton
Programmer
Joshua Hirsch
Creative Director
Michael Lebowitz
URL
www.wimbledonmovie.com/game/
Annual ID
05202N

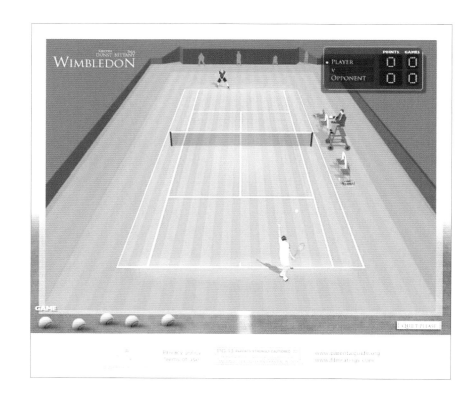

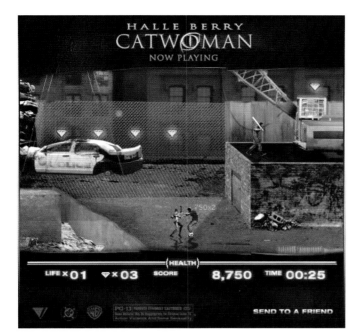

BRAND GAMING . WEB SITES

AGENCY
Big Spaceship/Brooklyn
CLIENT
Warner Bros

Art Director
D. Garrett Nantz
Writer
Karen Dahlstrom
Digital Artists/Multimedia
D. Garrett Nantz, David Chau
Programmers
Joshua Hirsch, Christian Stadler
Designers
D. Garrett Nantz, David Chau,
Michael Dillingham
Creative Director
Michael Lebowitz
URL
www.catwomanmovie.
com/game/
Annual ID
05203N

BRAND GAMING . WEB SITES

AGENCY
Farfar/Stockholm
CLIENT
Red Bull

Art Director
Jakob Swedenborg
Digial Artist/Multimedia
Anders Gustavsson
Programmer
Bo Gustavsson
Content Strategists
Per Näsholm, Matias Palm Jensen
Designers
Erik Norin, Per Hansson, Tim Sajdak
Creative Director
Nicke Bergström
URL
http://www.farfar.se/
OneShow2005/redbull_flakes
Annual ID
05205N

AGENCY
MTV Networks/New York
CLIENT
Nick Online

Art Director
Jamie Edis
Writer
Sean McEvoy
Digial Artist/Multimedia
Jamie Edis
Programmer
Simon Edis
Content Strategist
Sean McEvoy
Designer
Simon Edis
Information Architect
Simon Edis
Creative Director
Jason Root
URL
http://www.nick.com/games/
3d/sb_movie3D.jhtml
Username
nicknameX
Password
submit
Annual ID
05206N

AGENCY
MTV Networks/New York
CLIENT
Nick Online

Art Director
Richard Pasqua
Writer
Garrett Moehring
Programmer
Nate Altschul
Content Strategist
Richard Pasqua
Designer
Steve Hernandez
Information Architect
Richard Pasqua
Creative Director
Kyra Reppen
URL
www.nickjr.com/playtime/shows/
lazytown/games/lazy_getup.jhtml
Annual ID
05207N

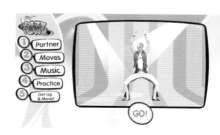

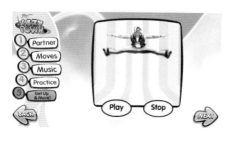

BRAND GAMING . WEB SITES

AGENCY
MTV Networks/New York
CLIENT
Nick Online

Art Director
Patrick Thiel
Writer
Sean McEvoy
Digial Artist/Multimedia
Tomasz Piasecki
Programmer
Patrick Thiel
Content Strategist
Sean McEvoy
Designer
Patrick Thiel
Information Architect
Patrick Thiel
Creative Director
Jason Root
URL
www.nick.com/games/data/
groove/bleep_2/playGame.jhtml
Username
nicknameX
Password
submit
Annual ID
05208N

BRAND GAMING . WEB SITES

AGENCY
MTV Networks/New York
CLIENT
Nick Online

Art Director
Richard Pasqua
Writer
Stepanie Sklar
Programmer
Nate Altschul
Content Strategist
Richard Pasqua
Designer
Steve Hernandez
Information Architect
Richard Pasqua
Creative Director
Kyra Reppen
URL
www.nickjr.com/playtime/
shows/dora/games/dora_
treasurehunt.jhtml
Annual ID
05209N

AGENCY
OgilvyInteractive/
Frankfurt am Main
CLIENT
PlayStation

Art Director
Thorsten Voigt
Writer
Andrea Goebel
Designer
Thorsten Voigt
Information Architect
Andrea Goebel
Creative Director
Michael Kutschinski
URL
www.ourwork.de/oneshow/
playstation/website
Annual ID
05210N

AGENCY
R/GA/New York
CLIENT
Nike

Writer
Steven Frischer
Digital Artists/Multimedia
Can Misirlioglu, Cesar De Castro
Programmers
Martin Legowiecki, Chuck Genco,
Stuart Buchbinder, Felix Turner,
Scott Prindle, Stan Wiechers
Content Strategists
Winston Binch, Matt Howell
Designers
David Hyung, Takafumi Yamaguchi,
Mikhail Gervits, Sacha Sedriks
Information Architect
Matt Walsh
Creative Directors
Rei Inamoto, Jason Marks
URL
awards.web.rga.com/2004/
gridiron.html
Annual ID
05211N

BRAND GAMING . WEB SITES

AGENCY
WM Team/Hannover
CLIENT
Continental AG

Art Director
Rainer Michael
Writer
Constantin Weimar
Programmer
Jens Franke
Content Strategist
Constantin Weimar
Designers
Jochen Kuckuck, Paul Stoll
Creative Director
Rainer Michael
URL
www.contifanworld.com/
?contentID=backFour
Username
oneshow
Password
interactive
Annual ID
05212N

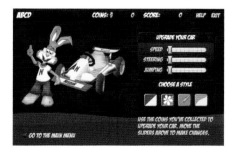

BRAND GAMING .
OTHER DIGITAL MEDIA

AGENCY
BLITZ/Beverly Hills
CLIENT
Nestlé Nesquik

Art Director
Tim Pixton
Writer
David Pass
Digital Artists/Multimedia
Robert Gale, Tim Pixton, Brian Sanchez
Programmer
Brian Robbins
Content Strategists
Ken Martin, David Pass
Designers
Ken Martin, Tim Pixton
Creative Director
Ken Martin
URL
www.nesquik.com/games/
xTremekart/Default.aspx
Annual ID
05213N

AGENCY
AgenciaClick/São Paulo
CLIENT
C&A Fashion

Art Directors
Sergio Stefano, Thiago Zanato
Writers
PJ Pereira, Suzana Apelbaum,
Jean Boechat, Haydee Uekubo
Programmer
Samuel Luchini
Designers
Samuel Luchini, Mauricio Reis,
Eduardo Marques, Jean Boechat
Creative Directors
PJ Pereira, Suzana Apelbaum
URL
www.virtualsofa.net/virtuallover
Annual ID
05214N

AGENCY
Atmosphere Cph/Copenhagen
CLIENT
Atmosphere Cph

Art Director
Søren Nørgaard
Programmer
Rasmus Hansen
Content Strategist
Tobias Smith-Fibiger
Designer
Søren Nørgaard
Creative Director
Carsten Gottschalck Vigh
URL
www.atmosphere-cph.com
Annual ID
05215N

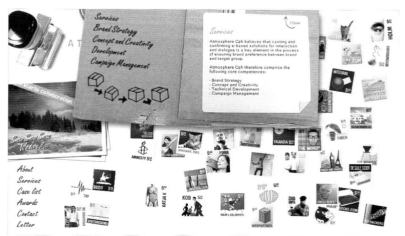

SELF-PROMOTION . WEB SITES

AGENCY
Dentsu (Interactive Salaryman)/
Tokyo
CLIENT
Takehiko Inoue
(Interactive Salaryman)

Art Director
Hirozumi Takakusaki
Writer
Nobuko Funaki
Digial Artist/Multimedia
Hiroki Nakamura
Designer
Yusuke Kitani
Creative Directors
Naoyuki Sato, Takehiko Inoue
URL
www.interactive-salaryman.com/
pieces/slamdunk_e/
Annual ID
05229N

AGENCY
Lateral/London
CLIENT
Lateral

Art Director
Simon Crab
Writer
David Jones
Programmer
Karsten Schmidt
Content Strategist
Karsten Schmidt
Designers
Karsten Schmidt, Karl Andersson
Information Architect
Karsten Schmidt
Director
Jon Bains
Creative Director
Simon Crab
URL
http://www.lateral.net
Annual ID
05219N

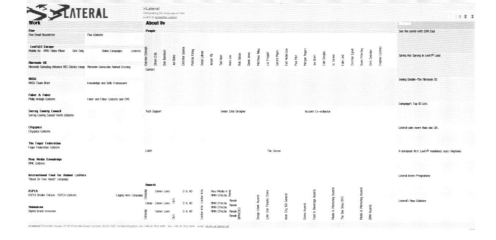

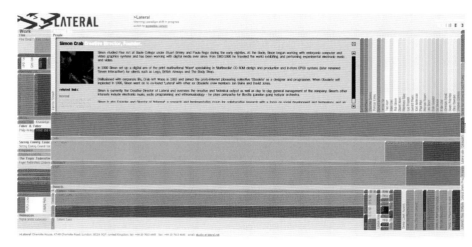

AGENCY
Neighbor/Singapore
CLIENT
Neighbor

Art Directors
Peh Chee Way, Shaun Sho
Writer
Kelvin Pang
Programmer
Tee You Meng
Designer
Lee Huei Yaw
Creative Directors
Peh Chee Way, Shaun Sho
URL
http://www.neighbor.com.sg
Annual ID
05220N

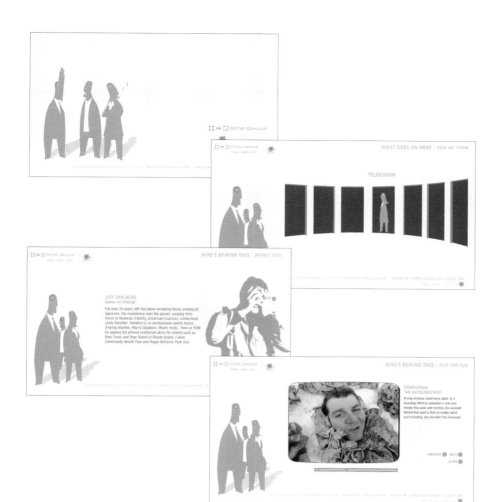

SELF-PROMOTION . WEB SITES

AGENCY
RDW Group/Providence
CLIENT
RDW Group

Art Director
Jeff Dahlberg
Writer
Wendy Boffi
Digital Artists/Multimedia
Max Pfennighaus, Jim Diotte
Programmers
Jim Franz, Chris Teso, Chopping Block
Content Strategist
Mike Doyle
Designers
Jeff Dahlberg, Max Pfennighaus,
Jim Diotte
Information Architect
Dennis Franczak
Creative Director
Jeff Patch
URL
www.rdwgroup.com
Annual ID
05222N

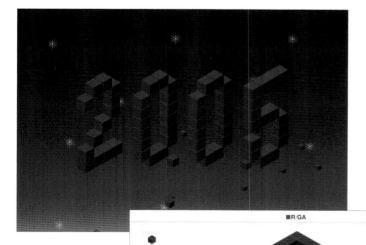

SELF-PROMOTION . WEB SITES

AGENCY
R/GA/New York
CLIENT
R/GA

Art Director
Emma Johns
Writer
Todd Brown
Digital Artist/Multimedia
Justin Van Slembrouck
Programmers
John Jones, Ted Warner,
Michael Black
Designers
Gui Borchert, Piper Darley,
Ernest Rowe, John James
Information Architect
Matt Walsh
Creative Director
Kris Kiger
URL
rga.com/holiday/holiday.html
Annual ID
05221N

AGENCY
RMG David/New Delhi
CLIENT
RMG David

Art Directors
Jiten Thukral, Sumir Tagra
Writer
Nirmal Pulickal
Digital Artists/Multimedia
Jiten Thukral, Sumir Tagra
Programmer
Amit Rampal
Content Strategist
Nirmal Pulickal
Designers
Jiten Thukral, Sumir Tagra
Information Architect
Sumir Tagra
Creative Director
Josy Paul
URL
http://www.rmgdavidindia.com
Annual ID
05223N

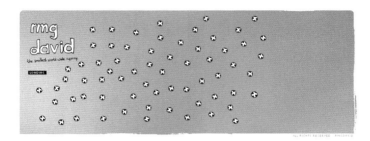

AGENCY
Scholz & Volkmer/Wiesbaden
CLIENT
Scholz & Volkmer

Writers
Andreas Henke, Michael Volkmer
Digial Artist/Multimedia
Ulrich Pohl
Programmers
Mario Dold, Thorsten Kraus,
Andreas Klinger,
Sascha Hillingshäuser
Creative Director
Heike Brockmann
URL
www.s-v.de/allesstrahlt
Annual ID
05224N

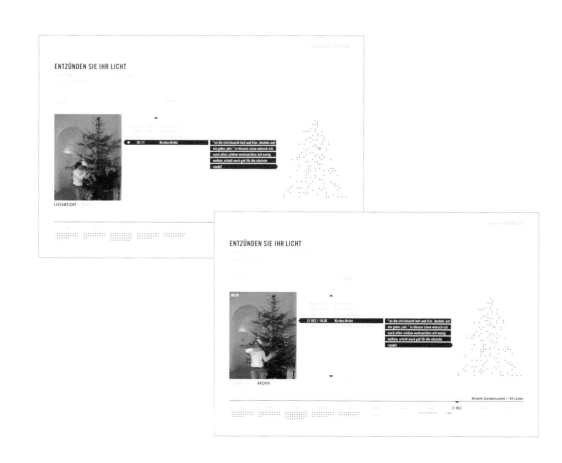

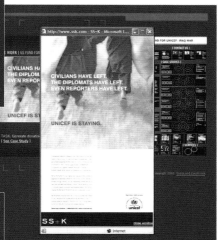

SELF-PROMOTION . WEB SITES

AGENCY
SS+K/New York
CLIENT
SS+K

Art Directors
Alice Ann Wilson, Cary Gibaldi
Writer
Marty Cooke
Programmer
Kevin Cancienne
Content Strategists
Kevin Slavin, Cary Gibaldi
Creative Director
Marty Cooke
URL
www.ssk.com
Annual ID
05225N

SELF-PROMOTION . WEB SITES

AGENCY
Tribal DDB/London
CLIENT
Tribal DDB

Art Director
Alex Braxton
Writers
Amy Gould, Ben Clapp
Digital Artists/Multimedia
James Robb, Nicole Schloeter
Programmer
Tristan Holman
Designer
Dieter Weichman
Information Architect
Tristan Holman
Creative Director
Ben Clapp
URL
http://www.tribalddb.co.uk/xmas/
Annual ID
05226N

AGENCY
Tribal DDB Australia/Sydney
CLIENT
Tribal DDB

Art Director
Mark Cracknell
Writer
Aaron Michie
Programmers
Terence Chang,
Ferdinand Haratua
Content Strategist
Aaron Michie
Designer
Ivan Yip
Creative Director
Aaron Turk
URL
www.tribalddb.com.au/
oneshow/tribalddb
Annual ID
05227N

AGENCY
Wieden + Kennedy/Portland
CLIENT
W+K 12

Art Director
W+K 12
Writer
W+K 12
Digital Artist/Multimedia
W+K 12
Programmer
W+K 12
Content Strategist
W+K 12
Designer
W+K 12
Information Architect
W+K 12
Creative Director
W+K 12
URL
www.wk12.com
Annual ID
05228N

NON-PROFIT . WEB SITES

AGENCY
ANIMAX/Culver City
CLIENT
Starlight Starbright
Children's Foundation

Art Director
Al Rosson
Writer
Starlight Starbright
Children's Foundation
Digial Artist/Multimedia
David Croy
Programmers
ANIMAX, DDM Group
Content Strategists
Michael Bellavia
Designer
Al Rosson, Dena Light
Information Architect
David Croy
Creative Directors
Al Rosson, Tim Jones
URL
www.slsb.org/chemo/
Annual ID
05230N

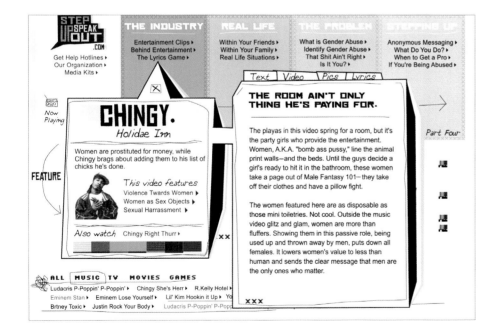

NON-PROFIT . WEB SITES

AGENCY
Archrival/Lincoln
CLIENT
Nebraska Domestic Violence
Council

Art Director
Clint! Runge
Writers
Clint! Runge, Allison Sagehorn
Digital Artists/Multimedia
Clint! Runge, Carey Goddard,
Bart Johnston
Programmers
Bart Johnston, Craig Kohtz
Content Strategist
Joe Goddard
Designer
Clint! Runge
Information Architect
Joe Goddard
Creative Director
Clint! Runge
URL
www.stepupspeakout.com
Annual ID
05231N

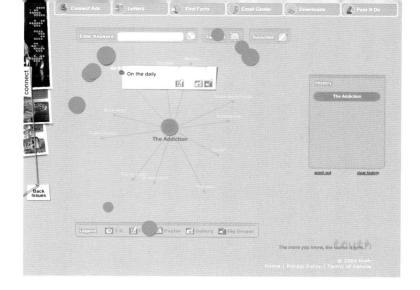

AGENCY
Arnold Worldwide/Boston
Crispin Porter + Bogusky/Miami
CLIENT
American Legacy Foundation

Art Director
Meghan Siegal
Writer
Mike Howard
Programmers
Doug Smith, Ebbey Mathew,
Adam Buhler
Designers
Meghan Siegal, Cindy Moon,
David Chung, Max Pfennighaus
Information Architect
Melissa Goldstein
Creative Directors
Ron Lawner, Pete Favat,
Alex Bogusky, Roger Baldacci,
Tom Adams
URL
www.connect-truth.com
Annual ID
05232N

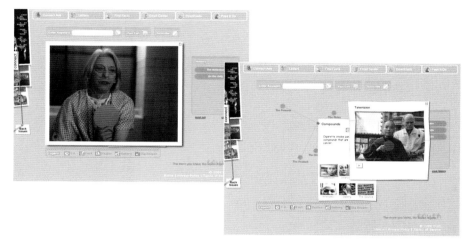

AGENCY
Arnold Worldwide/Boston
Crispin Porter + Bogusky/Miami
CLIENT
American Legacy Foundation

Art Director
Meghan Siegal
Writer
Marc Einhorn
Programmers
Ebbey Mathew, Adam Buhler
Designers
Max Pfennighaus, Jason Warne,
Meghan Siegal, Cindy Moon
Information Architect
Melissa Goldstein
Creative Directors
Ron Lawner, Pete Favat, Alex Bogusky,
Roger Baldacci, Tom Adams
URL
http://crazyworld.thetruth.com
Annual ID
05233N

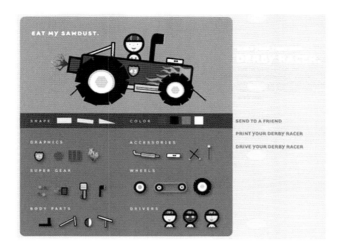

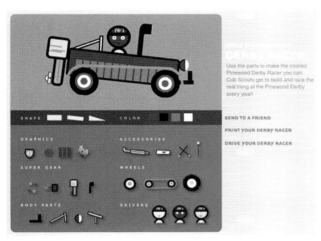

NON-PROFIT . WEB SITES

AGENCY
Carmichael Lynch/Minneapolis
CLIENT
Cub Scouts (Viking Indianhead
Council, BSA)

Writer
Bob Harrison
Programmer
Paul Nealy
Designer
James Christanson
Creative Directors
Glen Fellman, Jack Supple
URL
www.joincubs.com/games/
derby/derby.asp
Annual ID
05235N

NON-PROFIT . WEB SITES

AGENCY
Dentsu/Tokyo
CLIENT
National Federation of UNESCO
Associations in Japan

Art Director
Hirozumi Takakusaki
Writer
Fumihiko Sagawa
Digial Artist/Multimedia
Hiroki Nakamura
Designer
Yusuke Kitani
Creative Director
Hirozumi Takakusaki
URL
www.interactive-salaryman.com/
pieces/kururinpa_e/
Annual ID
05241N

AGENCY
Hunt Adkins/Minneapolis
CLIENT
American Cancer Society/
Blue Cross Blue Shield

Art Director
Steve Mitchell
Writer
Doug Adkins
Digial Artist/Multimedia
Images Designed
Programmer
Aaron Cooper
Content Strategists
Doug Adkins, Steve Mitchell
Designer
Aesthetic Apparatus
Information Architect
Images Designed
Creative Directors
Doug Adkins, Steve Mitchell
URL
www.walkingtimebomb.com
Annual ID
05236N

AGENCY
IconNicholson/New York
CLIENT
Project Rebirth

Art Director
Claudia Chow
Writer
Project Rebirth
Digial Artist/Multimedia
See-ming Lee
Programmers
Tim Murtaugh, Miles Kafka
Designers
Claudia Chow, See-ming Lee,
Chris Brugh
Information Architect
Larry Burks
Creative Director
Robert J Fisher
URL
www.projectrebirth.org
Annual ID
05237N

NON-PROFIT . WEB SITES

AGENCY
odopod/San Francisco
CLIENT
Nike/Lance Armstrong
Foundation

Art Director
Ammon Haggerty
Writer
Gwinn Appleby
Digital Artists/Multimedia
Laura Plageman, Ammon Haggerty
Programmers
Ammon Haggerty,
Michelangelo Capraro,
Alon Salant
Content Strategists
Gwinn Appleby, Jacquie Moss
Designers
Ammon Haggerty,
Michelangelo Capraro,
Chris Brown
Creative Directors
Tim Barber, Jacquie Moss,
David Bliss
URL
http://www.wearyellow.com
Annual ID
05238N

NON-PROFIT . WEB SITES

AGENCY
Tribal DDB Canada/Vancouver
CLIENT
BC Tobacco Reduction

Art Director
Bruce Sinclair
Writer
Kevin Shortt
Digital Artists/Multimedia
Koko Productions,
The Happy Endings (music)
Programmer
Dana Brousseau
Content Strategists
Kimberly Clifford, Michael Parker
Designer
Kelly Hale, Gerard Barcelon
Producer
Kimberly Clifford
Creative Director
Bruce Sinclair
URL
www.exhale.ca
Annual ID
05239N

AGENCY
Wunderman/Chicago
CLIENT
Motorola

Art Directors
Dean Caruso, Michael Rezac
Writer
Rebecca Zdarsky
Programmer
Chad Rupp
Content Strategist
Rebecca Zdarsky
Designer
Dean Caruso, Chad Rupp
Creative Director
Michael Rezac
URL
www.chicago.wunderman.com/
motorola/2005/Wundermoto/rdc/
index.htm
Username
Motorola
Password
xcellencce
Annual ID
05240N

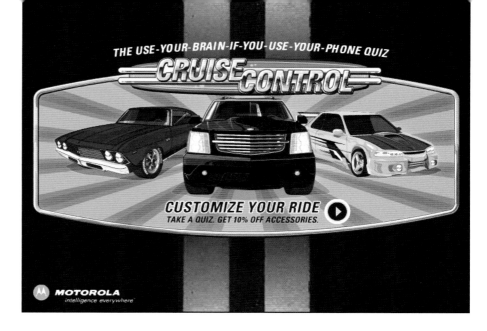

AGENCY
zentropy/Madrid
CLIENT
MSF Spain
(Doctors Without Borders)

Art Director
Rodrigo Jatene
Writer
Pepa Rojo
Programmers
Fernando Reig, Raul Fernández,
Tie Blumer
Content Strategist
Sebastián Méndez
Designer
Javier Burgueño
Creative Director
Kuki Bastos
URL
www.be-on.com/2005/
oneshow/MSF/cuento
Annual ID
05242N

ONE SIP LEADS TO ANOTHER.

ONE SIP LEADS TO ANOTHER.

ONE SIP LEADS TO ANOTHER.
FIND OUT HOW TO STOP.

ONE SIP LEADS TO ANOTHER.
FIND OUT HOW TO STOP.

NON-PROFIT . OTHER DIGITAL MEDIA

AGENCY
BatesAsia/Shanghai
CLIENT
China Forbidden Drunk-Driving
Association

Art Directors
Jody Xiong, Aif Xie
Writer
Ken Tao, Jody Xiong
Digial Artist/Multimedia
Jody Xiong
Programmer
Johnson Zhang
Content Strategist
Jody Xiong
Designers
Jody Xiong, Gavin Ning, Seven Yu
Creative Directors
Ken Tao, Jody Xiong
Annual ID
05243N

ALCOHOL CONSUMES YOUR ABILITY TO DRIVE!

CHINA FORBIDDEN DRUNK-DRIVING ASSOCIATION

NON-PROFIT . OTHER DIGITAL MEDIA

AGENCY
J. Walter Thompson/São Paulo
CLIENT
Alcoholics Anonymous

Art Director
Veni Cury
Writer
Suzana Apelbaum
Digial Artist/Multimedia
Rogerio Nogueira
Programmer
Rogerio Nogueira
Designer
Veni Cury
Creative Director
Suzana Apelbaum
URL
http://www.jwt.com.br/Awards_2005/
stop/en/
Annual ID
05244N

AGENCY
OgilvyInteractive/São Paulo
CLIENT
Parkinson Brazilian Association

Art Directors
Pedro Gravena, Danilo Janjacomo
Writers
Miguel Genovese, Cristiane Parede
Programmer
Vincent Maraschin
Designer
Márcio Holanda
Creative Directors
Marco Antônio de Almeida,
Adriana Cury
URL
www.ourwork.com.br/oldlady
Annual ID
05245N

AGENCY
Publicis Mojo/Auckland
CLIENT
Amnesty International

Art Director
Josh Moore
Writer
Seymour Pope
Digial Artist/Multimedia
Jeremy Clark
Programmer
Jeremy Clark
Content Strategist
Fleur Head
Designer
Department of Motion Picture Graphics
Information Architect
Jeremy Clark
Creative Director
Nick Worthington
Annual ID
05246N

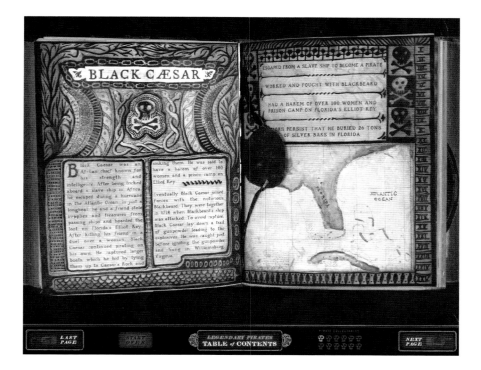

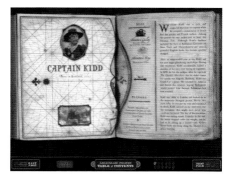

NON-PROFIT . OTHER DIGITAL MEDIA

AGENCY
Second Story Interactive Studios/
Portland
CLIENT
Pirate Soul Museum

Writers
Sharon Barry, Marti Johnson
Digital Artists/Multimedia
David Olson, Martin Linde,
David Waingarten, Carolyn Brewer
Programmers
Thomas Wester, David Knape
Content Strategist
Julie Beeler
Designer
Brad Johnson
Information Architect
Julie Beeler
Creative Director
Brad Johnson
URL
http://www.rainger.co.nz/amnesty/
Annual ID
05247N

29 m90

INDEX

CONTENT STRATEGIST

CREATIVE DIRECTOR

DIGITAL ARTIST/MULTIMEDIA

WRITER

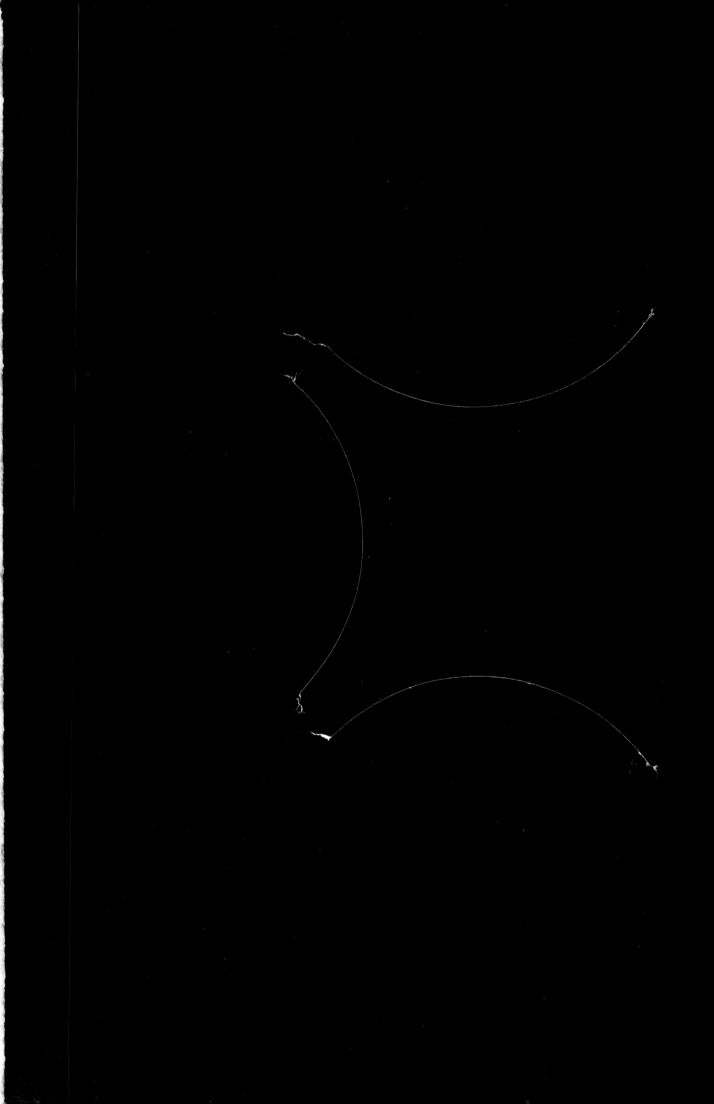

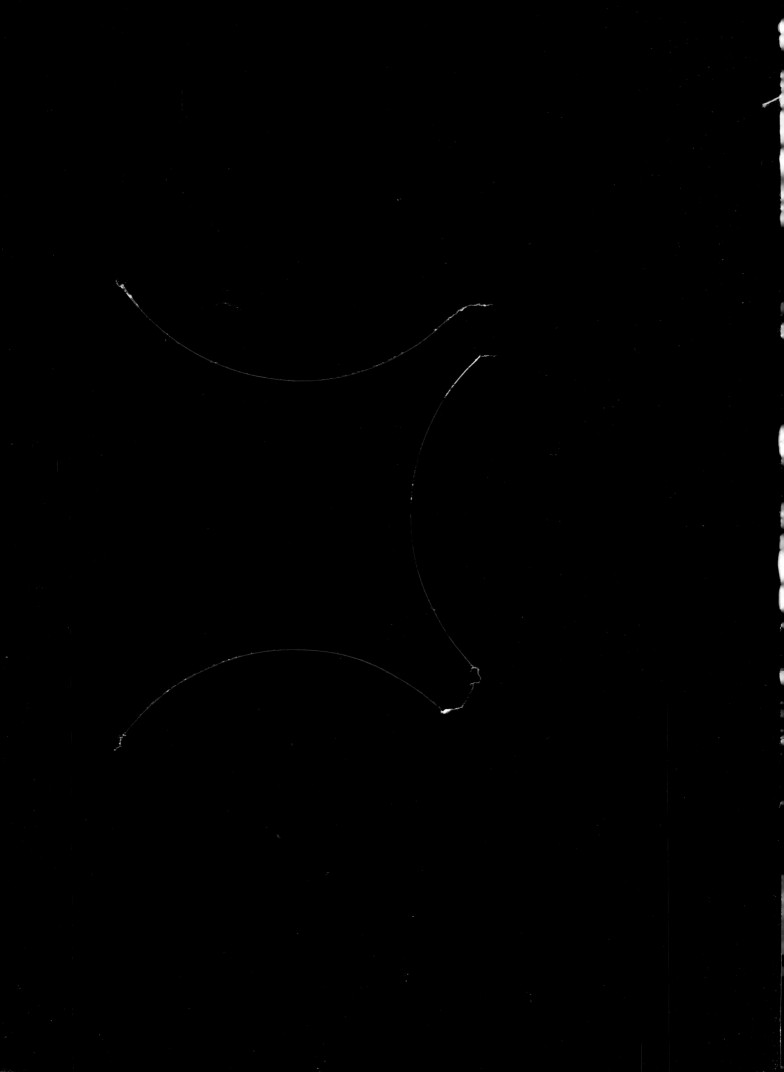